HOSEA

Unfailing Love Changes Everything

JENNIFER ROTHSCHILD

LifeWay Press®
Nashville, Tennessee

Published by LifeWay Press® • © 2015 Jennifer Rothschild

ISBN 9781430040200 • Item 005727067

Dewey decimal classification: 224.6
Subject headings: BIBLE, OT, HOSEA \ LOVE \ PROVIDENCE & GOVERNMENT OF GOD

To order additional copies of this resource, write to LifeWay Church Resources Customer Service; One LifeWay Plaza; Nashville, TN 37234-0113; order online at www.lifeway.com; fax 615.251.5933; phone toll free 800.458.2772; email orderentry@lifeway.com; or visit the LifeWay Christian Store serving you.

Printed in the United States of America

Adult Ministry Publishing • LifeWay Church Resources • One LifeWay Plaza • Nashville, TN 37234-0152

CONTENTS

HOSEA

ABOUT THE AUTHOR

Hosea: Unfailing Love Changes Everything is Jennifer's fifth video-based Bible study with LifeWay. It follows her popular Bible studies, *Missing Pieces: Real Hope When Life Doesn't Make Sense*, and *Me, Myself, and Lies: A Thought-Closet Makeover*.

Jennifer became blind when she was 15 years old and has experienced firsthand how God's unfailing love really does change everything. Now, more than 30 years later as an author and speaker, she boldly and compassionately teaches women how God's love can change them too.

Known for her substance, signature wit, and down-to-earth style, Jennifer weaves together colorful illustrations with biblical truths to help women know and live for Christ. She has shared her practical and inspiring messages to audiences across the country and through media outlets including *The Dr. Phil Show, Good Morning America, Life Today, The Learning Channel*, and *The Billy Graham Television Special*.

She is the featured teacher and founder of Fresh Grounded Faith Conferences and publisher of the popular online magazine for women in ministry called *womensministry.net*.

Jennifer and her husband, whom she calls her "very own Dr. Phil" live in Springfield, Missouri, and have two sons, Connor and Clayton, and a lovely daughter-in-law, Caroline. Besides walking—or being walked by—her little dog Lucy, Jennifer enjoys nature walks with her husband and riding a bicycle built for two.

She is also an avid listener of audio books, a C.S. Lewis junkie, and loves dark chocolate and robust coffee—especially when shared with a friend.

Connect with Jennifer at *JenniferRothschild.com/Hosea*.

INTRODUCTION

Hey girl! Thanks for choosing to get to know Hosea along with me. My dad used to tell me Hosea and Gomer's story when I was a child but, with his thick southern accent, I thought their names were "Hosear" and "Goma"!

No matter how you pronounce their names though, you will love their story; it's a story of unfailing love—God's unfailing love that changes everything. It transformed a prostitute to a treasured bride and a wayward woman to a restored wife. And it can change us too.

We're all a lot like Gomer—prone to wander. Maybe not unfaithful in marriage or other relationships, but we are all prone to wander from God and our identity in Him.

I've learned the hard way that when I wander away from God, I wonder who I am. But, through Hosea, I got a right view of God and I now have a right view of myself—a loved, accepted and complete woman of God. Oh sister, I want that for you too.

So, here's how we'll do this thing: you spend time with the Holy Spirit during the week doing the daily work. Your group will gather seven times. At each session, you'll say hey to your friends and get to know new ones. Your leader will welcome you and begin with prayer. Then, you'll let me join you through the video—and, I know that means you'll discuss for the first thirty seconds what I'm wearing! But, once you're done with that, I hope our time together will challenge you, comfort you, and clarify something about God or yourself that will help you know Him better and love Him more. After the video, your group will discuss what you've discovered in the homework. You'll find suggested questions on the group page for that week.

Also in the back of this book, in the word to leaders, I've tucked some "love gifts" your leader may want to provide. And you may need to help her out and pitch in to make the love gifts special for you, your leader, and your group each week. I've designed them to reinforce the teaching of Hosea and remind you how loved you are.

While we hang out, you'll hear me call you a "Gomer Girl." And, that is one of the sweetest names you can be called. To be a Gomer Girl means you are loved, accepted, and complete.

So, here we go … Gomer Girl!

Love, Jennifer

Group Session 1

Rather than a formal leader guide in the back, we've provided what we hope is a simple and functional group plan on these pages with an additional word to leaders in back. Each week will begin with a two-page group guide like this. I suggest that you divide your group time into three parts: 1. Welcome and prayer; 2. Watch the video; 3. Group discussion of the study for the past week and the video.

   The session guide for this first meeting is for us to get to know each other. Then we'll each go do our homework (it will be fun, I promise). Each day, plan to spend a few minutes with that day's study. Don't worry if some days you don't get it all. This isn't a race and you can come back later. When we meet next group session, we'll have this week's study to discuss. Now let's get to know each other and I'll join you by way of video.

BEFORE THE VIDEO
Welcome and Prayer

VIDEO NOTES
Four Ingredients in Hosea

1. _____ himself

   • Hosea was a _____ who served Israel in the eighth century, B.C.

   • Hosea's name means "_____."

2. Our friend, _____

   • Gomer means "_____, the filling up of idolatry."

   • Gomer's marriage to Hosea represents Israel's _____ relationship with God.

3. _____

Find Jennifer's mint recipe at
JenniferRothschild.com/Hosea

4. _____ and _____

   • God chose to _____ us just like He chose to love Israel. And we, too, are
     prone to _____.

Four Ways to See Yourself in the Book of Hosea

   1. *My* _____—covenant name

   2. _____—national identity

   3. _____—affectionate nickname

   4. _____—influencer

The main character of the Book of Hosea is _____ _____.

CONVERSATION GUIDE
Video 1 and Getting to Know Each Other

What is one thing you want your group to know about you?

What drew you to this study?

What do you think of when someone mentions the Book of Hosea?

Do you have a favorite verse or idea from Hosea? If so what?

HOSEA

CONNECT WITH JENNIFER AT

JenniferRothschild.com/Hosea

We are the ones God chose and loves.
#HoseaStudy

JUST BECAUSE LOVE

HOSEA

Day 1
THIS IS YOUR STORY

The word of the LORD that came to Hosea son of Beeri during
the reigns of Uzziah, Jotham, Ahaz, and Hezekiah, kings of
Judah, and of Jeroboam son of Jehoash, king of Israel.

HOSEA 1:1

You're about to experience a salacious story about an unlikely couple, an unusual marriage, a man in love, and an illicit affair. But this affair was not the end of the marriage; it was the beginning of a love story. A love story that will take your breath away.

This story overflows with failure, selfishness, despair, forgiveness, second chances, and restoration. And you thought this was a Bible Study.

It is! The Book of Hosea is one of the most beautiful and confusing books you will ever read. The story of Hosea and his wife will shock you and warm your heart. The story of Israel and God in the book of Hosea will frustrate you and then fill you with hope.

You will discover that the Book of Hosea is the story of God and Israel, Hosea and Gomer, and … the story of you. This is your love story.

But, for all its beauty, trying to explain Hosea just about did me in! How do you explain such contrasts of hope and judgment, loyalty and betrayal? I tried to understand it. I tried to organize it. I tried to explain it. Finally, I just had to sit in wonder at the feet of Hosea and his God.

So, I'll tell you right up front—I had no idea how to teach this book!

But, after praying, writing, starting over, rewriting, crying to my editor, and trying some more to find a way to communicate it, I finally found the answer resting on my husband's nose.

Let me explain.

My husband, Phil, got trifocals when he turned 50. If you know my story, you will smile when I tell you that having to wear trifocals at fifty is not one of my issues! (If you don't know why that's funny, read my bio!) Even though I don't have first-hand experience with those eyeglasses, here's what I know about them.

Trifocals help you focus in three distinct areas: distance, intermediate, and near vision. And that's how you need to view Hosea, too. So, girl, put on your spiritual trifocals—we're going to dive into the Book of Hosea. The first time I read the Book of Hosea,

I didn't see it through those three distinct lenses, and it was pretty blurry. As soon as I focused on what seemed like God's love, I would blink and the very next verse was His judgment. Huh? Then, I would refocus and think I was seeing Hosea's and Gomer's love story just to be rubbing my eyes trying to see whom Hosea was talking about. What? It was so confusing.

That's why you need trifocals to see Hosea's book clearly. When you put on your trifocals, you will see these three views:

DISTANCE: According to Phil, when he looks through the top of his trifocals, he can see what is farther away. He uses this part of the lens to drive so he can get a view of the road ahead and find the closest Starbucks® for his coffee-loving wife. So, when you view Hosea from a distance, you can see the historical landscape of Israel at the time of King Jeroboam's reign when the Israelites were prosperous but unfaithful. You get to see the prophet Hosea in action, preaching sermons of judgment and hope to God's rebellious people.

INTERMEDIATE: The middle section of Phil's trifocals help him see what's at arm's length. He's constantly peering through this part to work on his computer or watch Georgia football on TV. So, when you view Hosea at arm's length, you can get a better view of Hosea the husband, his wife, and their family situation. Remember this basic orientation: Hosea's book is a sermon and his life is the illustration. His love for his unfaithful wife reflects God's redemptive love for Israel.

NEAR: This is the bottom part of Phil's trendy Warby Parker-framed trifocals and it lets him use close-up vision for reading his wife's books or threading a needle to sew on his own missing buttons because he is a major-stud husband. So, for us, this is the lens through which you read Hosea to see what's right under your nose. It helps you see yourself in the story of Israel. It allows you to see yourself in the story of Hosea and Gomer. With this view, you can see who you are and how dearly loved you are. It lets you see that Hosea is your love story.

Oh, you will be so glad you chose to get to know Hosea! And I'm so glad to have you along with me. If you sometimes feel lost or disoriented though, you're in good company. I'm there too. But Dr. Phil tells me that's part of getting used to trifocals. If you turn your head too fast you may feel dizzy. In those moments hang onto the main theme of Hosea. God loves us so much that even when we've betrayed His love, He comes looking for us.

He buys us back, takes us home, cleans us up, and keeps loving us. Who wouldn't endure a little dizziness for a love like that?

OK. Ready? Let's get oriented. When you look at the Book of Hosea through your trifocals, you will see that the whole book is set within a literary style frame. Hosea was a prophet but he was also a master literary craftsman. His style is eloquent and picturesque—full of simile and metaphor. Great preachers use great illustrations. So Hosea starts his sermon with the guiding visual of his marriage to Gomer. Yes, that is really her name. What were her parents thinking?

Chapters 1–3 are basically a narrative combining prose and poetry. Then, Hosea changes tempo. Chapters 4–14 take the form of ancient Hebrew poetry. They contain most of the story of Israel's failure and God's faithfulness. Some of it is blow-you-away beautiful, some of it is so artsy that it's hard to follow, and then some of it is quite honestly rated PG-13—a bit graphic.

But, the poetry of Hosea serves a purpose. Now, if you have painful memories of some poetry class, or if the only poet you've ever read is Dr. Seuss, please indulge me anyway for a moment. Let me ask you a question.

Why do you think we value poetry even when we may struggle to understand it?

What kinds of ideas do you think poetry can convey that prose cannot?

Don't stress with those questions. I don't know the answers fully either, but I just want you to think about it.

I think we love poetry because prose clearly states, but poetry suggests. With poetry, our hearts understand even when our minds can't explain it. Prose might say "I love you, you're beautiful," while poetry might say:

> Oh, that he would kiss me with the kisses of his mouth!
> For your love is more delightful than wine.
> The fragrance of your perfume is intoxicating;
> Your name is perfume poured out.
> **SONG OF SONGS 1:2-3**

Ahhh! Beautiful, isn't it? Now that you have an idea what is in Hosea, adjust your spiritual trifocals and take about 30 minutes to read Hosea. It's only 14 chapters and it won't take you long. Don't get overwhelmed if you get confused. It is confusing! It's not written in a linear fashion. Just try to generally think, is this part talking about God's love and judgment toward Israel, is it about Hosea and Gomer, or is it timeless truth that applies to me? Don't be surprised if some verses make you question why God seems harsh. Also, don't be surprised if after you read a verse that suggests God is done with His people, He turns around a verse later and shows such tenderness that you have to wipe away your own tears. Don't worry, it will make sense by the time we grow through it together. All you are trying to accomplish with this first read-through is familiarity with the book. That's all. So don't stress out. Pour yourself some tea, snuggle up with your new favorite prophet, and enjoy!

Besides, you look absolutely adorable in trifocals!

Happy reading!

HOSEA

Day 2
THE BACK STORY

When the LORD first spoke to Hosea, He said this to him:
Go and marry a promiscuous wife
and have children of promiscuity,
for the land is committing blatant acts of promiscuity
by abandoning the LORD.
HOSEA 1:2

Dizzy yet?

I ask you if you're dizzy because I figure you've read Hosea by now. And, if you have, I wonder if you felt any of the feelings I did. Feelings like awe, confusion, dismay, affection, and frustration. Dizzying, isn't it?

Jot down some adjectives that come to mind when you think of what you read in Hosea.

In a few weeks, when you are an expert on Hosea (wink, wink), we'll come back to this page and see if your adjectives change. I have to be honest. When I read the whole book through the first several times, two adjectives that came to mind were judgmental and harsh. I don't like those words. But, the longer I've studied Hosea, my adjectives changed to words like tender, restorative, and compassionate.

So, if you got a dim view of the message of Hosea when you read it the first time, stay with me, sister. I promise you will understand it better and love it more as we go. What I discovered is that Hosea helped me know myself better and love God more. Don't you want that too? I think you'll experience the same, you'll see.

I can't think of a clever beginning, so without flowery fanfare, let's just do this thing. The rest of this week, we will unpack chapter one so let's start with verse one and get oriented to the place and time Hosea preached.

> The word of the LORD that came to Hosea son of Beeri during
> the reigns of Uzziah, Jotham, Ahaz, and Hezekiah, kings of
> Judah, and of Jeroboam son of Jehoash, king of Israel.
> **HOSEA 1:1**

Now, if you started to glaze over by the third name in that list of unfamiliar people, don't worry; I'll tell you what all those names represent! Hosea was a prophet who ministered to Israel, the Northern Kingdom, during the reign of King Jeroboam—let's call him KJ2, okay? And the listing of all those unfamiliar kings indicates that, as Charles Dickens would say, "It was the best of times, it was the worst of times."[1] If you're not one who glazes over when you read historical detail and want more context, check out the article on the history of this story. Or, you can skip the article in the interest of being expeditious.

THE HISTORY OF THIS STORY

Hosea preached in, and to, the Kingdom of Israel (a.k.a. the Northern Kingdom, or the 10 northern tribes) during their final years as a nation. Under kings David and Solomon, Israel had been united. But after Solomon died, during the reign of his son Rehoboam (931 B.C.), Israel split into two kingdoms. The result was kind of like what you would imagine if the US Civil War ended differently, instead of the "United" States of America, there would be the Northern States of America and a Southern States of Dixie—two different, and not very friendly, nations crammed together as neighbors.

In Hosea's day, the Southern Kingdom was called Judah and its capitol was Jerusalem. The Northern Kingdom was called Israel and its capitol was Samaria, which was located in the tribe of Ephraim. So, when you read references to Israel or Ephraim or Samaria in Hosea, they're all referring to the Northern Kingdom. These 10 tribes were eventually conquered by Assyria and destroyed in 722 B.C.

After the Northern and Southern Kingdoms split up, Jeroboam I became Israel's first king (926-909 B.C.). He set up shrines for the people to worship calves at Bethel and Dan (see 1 Kings 12:25-30) as a way to sever the religious ties with Jerusalem. As a result, the Israelites descended into idol worship—this became known as the "sin of Jeroboam" (see 1 Kings 16:25-31).

---

1. Charles Dickens, *Tale of Two Cities* (Mineola, NY: Dover Publications, 1999), 1.

HOSEA

The King Jeroboam in Hosea 1:1 was King Jeroboam II (793-753 B.C., no relation to the earlier calf-making king). He ruled over Israel when the nation was prosperous. But, once KJ2 died, it became the worst of times. The kings who followed KJ2 were each assassinated or had short reigns until, eventually, Israel was conquered in 722 B.C. So Hosea's ministry spanned both the best of times and the worst of times.

Hosea's stern preaching was warning Israel that judgment was coming.

While Hosea preached in Israel, Isaiah and Amos were preaching in Judah. Hosea's ministry came before, and possibly overlapped, Micah's ministry to Israel. Those four prophets—Hosea, Amos, Isaiah, and Micah—are known as the great eighth century prophets.

KJ2 ruled over Israel for 40 years and the nation was outwardly doing great. In the ancient world, a long-ruling king meant stability and security. KJ2 had ended the wars his father began so Israel was at peace. He took back territory that had been lost, so Israel was prosperous. KJ2 had also increased commerce and wealth for Israel so they took a lot of pride in their affluence.

See why it was the best of times? But, that's not all. It was also the worst of times. Spiritually and morally, they were a wreck. The worship of God had descended into idolatry and empty ritualism. The country's leaders were corrupt, and crime had soared. Most serious of all, God's judgment was about to fall. See why it was the worst of times?

Look at it for yourself. How did the Bible describe the people of Israel in Hosea 4:1?

Well, that sums it up. They were unfaithful, showed no love, and didn't even acknowledge Yahweh. They may have been financially prosperous, but they were spiritually bankrupt. God loved Israel and wanted them to understand how grave their spiritual choices were, how painful and serious. So, he told the prophet Hosea to do something radical.

Look at Hosea 1:2, what did God tell Hosea to do?
□ shave his head and march through the city preaching repentance
□ marry a prostitute
□ fast for 40 days and pray for the people
□ burn down the high places to show God's displeasure with His people

Whoa! God told a man of God to marry a woman of many men, a woman of harlotry? Welcome to your first shock in the Book of Hosea. Some smart people who study this kind of stuff think this woman could have actually been a prostitute before Hosea married her. Some think she was simply a promiscuous woman. Some think she could have become promiscuous, committed adultery, and, then, become a prostitute after she married. I only mention those minor details because to some, those possibilities are important distinctions. To me, she was a sinner before, during, and after her marriage—and that's enough for me to really relate to her.

Her name was Gomer. I know, I know. Poor girl.

Look at the first phrase in Hosea 1:3 and jot down her father's name.

His name was Diblaim and it meant "double portion of raisin cakes" which were like an aphrodisiac—extra strength Viagra®. That should give you a hint of what Gomer's life must have been like. And, it also won't surprise you that the meaning of Gomer's name was "completion," as in the filling up of the measure of idolatry or fully ripened wickedness. Let's just say Gomer probably wasn't every mama's dream for her little boy! But God chose her for Hosea.

Why did God tell Hosea to marry a woman like her? Read Hosea 1:2.

Their marriage was to serve as a picture of God's relationship with Israel. So, let's leave Gomer for a minute and deal with Israel's back story so we can better understand Gomer's. The nation was called Israel and they were God's chosen people. This is how the book of Deuteronomy describes Israel:

> For you are a holy people to the LORD your God; the LORD your God
> has chosen you to be a people for His own possession out of all the
> peoples who are on the face of the earth. The LORD did not set His love
> on you nor choose you because you were more in number than any of
> the peoples, for you were the fewest of all peoples, but because the
> LORD loved you and kept the oath which He swore to your forefathers,
> the LORD brought you out by a mighty hand and redeemed you from
> the house of slavery, from the hand of Pharaoh king of Egypt.
> DEUTERONOMY 7:6-8 (NASB)

Wow. What an identity, huh? God chose and loved Israel—just because. He set His love upon them not because of what they did or how great they were, but just because God chose to. Now, back to Gomer.

If Hosea's marriage to Gomer is a picture of God's relationship with Israel, what does that say about Hosea's marriage to Gomer?

Hosea didn't set his love upon her because of what she did or how great she was or was not, he just chose to love her. Keep this in mind because in Hosea, Gomer is a picture of Israel, and Gomer is a picture of you and me too. We too are chosen and loved—that is our identity. But Israel and Gomer didn't always live like they were the chosen and loved. Israel was not behaving according to its identity. They were giving themselves to idols and had forsaken the Lord.

Why do you think Israel went for false gods when they were loved by the true God?

Why do you think Gomer went for other lovers even after she had the love of Hosea and identity as his bride?

Look at Hosea 13:6. What is God saying about His people that may help you answer those questions?

God provided for Israel and, when they were satisfied, they became proud and forgot God. What about you? Is it easier to forget God when He has blessed you with a life that is good and easy?

OK, here's another thing to consider. Read Hosea 11:7 to see how this verse may also influence your answers to those questions. What does it say the reason for Israel's and Gomer's unfaithfulness was?

"My people are bent on turning from Me."

They, we, are prone to wander—prone to leave the God we love.

You may not identify yourself as a harlot or adulterer, but do you consider yourself "prone to wander"? You may have had a better upbringing than Gomer or made better choices than Israel made. But what about your tendency toward tilting from God—wandering away from Him?

On the scale below, mark how prone, or bent, you are to wander and turn away from God:

NOT AT ALL   1   2   3   4   5   6   7   8   9   10   EXTREMELY

Well, if you marked anything below 5, let me clue you into something you may not really understand about yourself and your Gomer tendencies. The prophet Isaiah (who, by the way, served the Southern Kingdom of Judah at the same time Hosea served the Northern Kingdom of Israel) will tell you for me.

In Isaiah 53:6, to what does he compare us?

He compared us to sheep who have each gone our own way. We all have the tendency to get satisfied, get proud, and forget God. We all can wander and turn away. Really, we could all mark the 10 on that scale above.

HOSEA

Wandering from God does not have to happen on the grand Gomer scale and include words like "adultery" to be real and dangerous.

We can stray slightly by looking to another for our approval. We can find something, or someone, who satisfies our need for acceptance or identity; an object or activity that gives us a happy buzz. That is what Israel did when they wandered away from their identity and their God and turned to idols instead.

Israel's identity was a chosen and loved people of God. Your identity is a chosen and loved woman of God. Those of us who belong to God are God's people. We are chosen and loved by Him—that is our true identity.

But, when we wander from God, we will wonder who we are. And, when we wonder who we are, we will wander further from God to find out. We will wander off to other places and people to find our identity.

We are Gomer. We are the ones God chose and loves, but who are bent on turning from Him, chasing after other gods.

That's the story of us, isn't it? God entered the slave market where all of us were putting ourselves up for auction, prostituting ourselves and our humanity to a lesser life. On the cross Jesus paid the full price for our freedom. He bought us back. This is the scandal of God's love—His loving desire to make us His people and the full persons He intended us to be so that we would know our God, know our identity, know His love, and live the beautiful end of our story.

Day 3
THE BAD NEWS

So he went and married Gomer daughter of Diblaim, and she
conceived and bore him a son. Then the LORD said to him:
Name him Jezreel, for in a little while
I will bring the bloodshed of Jezreel
on the house of Jehu
and put an end to the kingdom of the house of Israel.
HOSEA 1:3-4

Well, you've got the basics of Hosea's story so far: Spiritual guy pursued scandalous girl. Sincere guy dated skeptical girl. God-centered guy married self-centered girl. Devalued daughter became highly valued bride. Aimless woman became a chosen wife.

And, now, I have an announcement … Hosea and Gomer are going to be parents!

Before we break the passage down, grant me a mushy Hallmark card moment. I know I am about to romanticize it, but it will help us get inside this story.

Think about it … Gomer had probably never experienced such stability. Because Hosea valued her, she began to feel her own value. She was no longer known as "Gomer the prostitute." She was known as "Gomer, the chosen and loved bride." Her identity had changed; her life was changing. And it should be no surprise, because Hosea's name means "salvation." Gomer must have known better than anyone that the meaning of his name fit him, for Hosea saved her—saved her from her past, from her insecurity, from fear for the future. He was her salvation.

So it should have been a happy and hopeful experience to become a mother, right? Well, you be the judge of that.

Now, imagine with me that you live in ancient Israel in 700 B.C. and Hosea is your pastor. You and all your girlfriends from church have been waiting for the last 9 months for this baby to come. It took a while for everyone at church to get used to the fact that Hosea actually chose Gomer, but finally, the church seemed to settle into the idea that if Hosea chose her, they would accept her.

Hosea, the new dad, gets up behind the pulpit and says, "Well, we have a new little guy here at church today." The grandmas in the congregation exhale, you sigh, and you

can hear the women around you coo. People are smiling until Hosea announces the name of their son.

What does Hosea 1:3-4 say Hosea named him?

Jezreel. Because you know the history and customs of ancient Israel in 700 B.C., you know this is not happy news! You know the child's name means God's about to "punish the house of Jehu for the bloodshed of Jezreel." And, you look over at your girlfriend because, uh, this Jehu and Jezreel stuff applies to you ... your people. If you want to know Jezreel's significance, read below.

Think of it this way. What if your pastor told you God was so tired of your unfaithfulness that He was going to cut off your blessings and protection? How would you feel?

WHAT'S A JEZREEL?

The significance of Jezreel began in Naboth's vineyard (1 Kings 21; 2 Kings 9). King Ahab and his wife, Queen Jezebel, were unbelievably wicked and they wanted Naboth's land—a vineyard in Jezreel. So, the pair trumped up charges, had Naboth executed, and stole his land. In judgment of their wicked ways, God sent a man named Jehu to kill both King Ahab and Queen Jezebel.

Jehu then became the new king of Israel. King Jehu killed all the descendants of Ahab (2 Kings 10:11) and this was known as the "blood of Jezreel."

You may have heard of Jezreel by another name. The area was also where Israel fought many great battles. Maybe you've heard of Megiddo?

I would feel completely terrified. I think of the Psalm: "Whom have I in heaven but you?" (Ps. 73:25, NASB). I have nothing without Him. I can't imagine hearing that message from God.

Well, if that isn't awful enough, what exactly does God say He will do in verse 5?

God says He will "break the bow of Israel in the Valley of Jezreel." That is like God saying, "I'm going to wipe out your army," or "I will destroy your weapons, so your enemies will defeat you in every battle."

Put yourself back in the congregation listening to Hosea again. You showed up for church expecting an encouraging sermon with three points and a funny story, and instead you got a baby dedication which morphed into the terrifying message that God will become your enemy, destroy your land, and maybe kill you in the bargain. Ouch.

What kinds of thoughts do you think would rush through your head if you heard on good authority that God was ready to walk away from you—not only turn away from you, but rise up against you?

I would feel completely unhinged and a little sick just imagining that was possible. Linger on that thought, because you cannot overstate the impact of Hosea's prophecy on the people that day. It was months later that Jezreel started crawling and getting into everything. Gomer started to feel a little queasy and bought a pregnancy test.

Nine months later ... it's a girl. What was her name? (Hosea 1:6)

Name her No Compassion,
For I will no longer have compassion
on the house of Israel.
I will certainly take them away.
HOSEA 1:6

Can you even imagine God not having compassion on His people? On you? *Compassion* means *to suffer with someone*. When the Bible says God is compassionate, it means He feels our hurt. He knows our suffering.

What feelings come to mind when you imagine God having no compassion on you?

For me, I would feel valueless, isolated, and vulnerable. Can it get any worse than God declaring He will have no compassion on you? Apparently it can.

What does verse 7 say?

While God will have no compassion on Israel, He will have compassion for their rivals in Judah. God will deliver Judah. Now that was just adding insult to injury. Oh girl, this is where God can seem so harsh if we don't view this book and His character correctly. So hold on. Believe the best about Him and you will see the best of Him.

Back to Hosea and Gomer. The family was growing. Gomer was a mother and Hosea was a father—they were human—just like you and me. They loved their children and God loved them too. Though we take this story literally, do not apply the literal meaning of the kid's names to the children as if God is rejecting them, or removing His compassion from them personally and individually. Their names were just part of the word picture God was communicating through Hosea and their family. The kids were like little walking reminders of the message Hosea was preaching to the nation of Israel.

Speaking of children, can you say, "Third time's a charm"? Gomer got pregnant again and their last son's name was not any better. Read what it was in Hosea 1:8-9.

The boy's name was to convey the idea that God's tolerance was about to run out and He would no longer call His people His own.

"Then the LORD said:
Name him Not My People,
for you are not My people,
and I will not be your God."
HOSEA 1:9

So now you're leaving the First Local Church of Hosea in Israel and you aren't feeling so hot. You've just heard the third of three really troubling sermons. Every time you see Hosea and Gomer's little ones toddling and crawling about, you can't help but remember what their names mean. You meet your friends at Yoshi's Grill for lunch and you discuss the sermon series with them. You take turns stating what Hosea has told you:

You say, "God will strip us of our security?"

Your friend adds, "And God will fight against us and make us powerless?"

Your friend's husband chimes in, "But God will harden His heart against us and have no compassion for us or our suffering."

Your mother finishes, "Yeah, God will disown us. If we come to Him for help, He will act like He doesn't know us."

Your server, who has been topping off your waters, interrupts and asks, "Really, God would do that? God is like that?"

This part of Hosea could hardly be more countercultural. God as angry? God as judge? God punishing His people?

Hard to swallow with that tasty lunch, isn't it?

How would you respond to that server who wonders if God would really do what Hosea claimed? (You don't have to know the answer; it's not an easy question.)

I guess what I may tell that server is this: God is a consuming fire. The same fire that could swallow up a sinner is the same fire that wants to melt your heart. Turn to Him, not from Him.

I can't tie a pretty bow on this part of Hosea to finish our time together; it's just plain bleak. So let me leave you with some good news from the last chapter of Hosea for you to ponder as you try to digest all this hard stuff.

[God said,] "I will heal their waywardness
and love them freely,
for my anger has turned away from them."
HOSEA 14:4 (NIV)

Good news is coming—I promise—so go have dessert!

HOSEA

Day 4
THE GOOD NEWS

> But I will have compassion on the house of Judah,
> and I will deliver them by the LORD their God.
> I will not deliver them by bow, sword, or war,
> or by horses and cavalry.
>
> **HOSEA 1:7**

Finally, right? Man, Hosea can be hard and we're only halfway through chapter one. But today will make you smile. In fact, most of this amazing book will make you smile … you'll see. Yesterday, we got a big serving of God's judgment and it sure didn't go down easy. God's people had betrayed Him, again and again. And through Hosea, Yahweh was warning His people that His patience was running out. He promised—and eventually sent—destruction.

Within only a few short years, Israel went from its highest pinnacle of success to complete destruction. The destruction that Hosea was warning against is detailed in 2 Kings 17:5-18 if you want to read more.

Hosea wasn't kidding around. But if you only get the judgment, you're missing the message of Hosea.

Turn in Hosea to chapter 1. We're going to unpack from Hosea 1:10 to Hosea 2:1. Some of the beauty of Hosea is in the breathtaking contrasts. But, though beautiful, they may give you whiplash. Remember, yesterday, with the names of his kids, Hosea just declared God had "no compassion" and "you're not [His] people." Watch how he follows the bitter with the sweet.

> Yet the number of the Israelites
> will be like the sand of the sea,
> which cannot be measured or counted.
> And in the place where they were told:
> You are not My people,
> they will be called: Sons of the living God.
> And the Judeans and the Israelites

will be gathered together.
They will appoint for themselves a single ruler
and go up from the land.
For the day of Jezreel will be great.
Call your brothers: My People
and your sisters: Compassion."
HOSEA 1:10–2:1

Did you catch how these verses are the sweet aftertaste to the bitter bites you had to digest from the first part of chapter 1?

v. 4	"an end to the kingdom of Israel"
v. 6-7	"I will no longer have compassion on the House of Israel… but I will have compassion on the house of Judah."
v. 7	"I will not deliver them"
v. 9	"not my people"
v. 10	"will be called: Sons of the living God."
v. 10	"you will be like sand of the sea"
v. 11	"gathered together" "a single ruler" "will be great"
v. 11	"the Judeans and the Israelites will be gathered together"

Though this is restorative and beautiful, Hosea speaks in radical contrasts, doesn't he? I'll just remind you that it isn't written in a linear fashion—it jumps around kinda like a long-tailed cat on a porch full of rocking chairs. Hosea snuggles absolute opposites together in the same chapter—in some places, in the same verse.

But even if the writing style puts what seems to be opposite words from God situated next to each other, it still doesn't explain why those opposite words are there in the first place. Which is it, God? Are they your people or not?

Or, closer to home, am I your daughter or not? After all, I blow it, too; I sin and turn away. If we wander off, does God disown us? Are we still His people?

Let God answer that question for you. His answer is in Hosea 11:8-9.
When you read it, insert your name where you read words like "Ephraim" and "Israel."

How can I give you up, _____ (Ephraim)?
How can I surrender you, _____ (Israel)?
How can I make you like Admah?
How can I treat you like Zeboyim?
I have had a change of heart;
My compassion is stirred!
I will not vent the full fury of My anger;
I will not turn back to destroy _____ (Ephraim).
For I am God and not man—
the Holy One among you;
I will not come in rage.

HOSEA 11:8-9

God will not give you up because you are His.

God chose Israel, Hosea chose Gomer, and God chose you. He loves you because of who He is—"I am God and not man, the Holy One among you."

God may discipline His people but He will not disown them.

The language God used in the first half of chapter 1 shows God is disciplining His people, not disowning them.

What does 2 Kings 17:13 specify that God was doing through the harsh words of Hosea and the other prophets?

All through Hosea, there's both judgment and hope, destruction and restoration. Hosea's preaching proclaims both sides of God, but the two faces of God we see in Hosea reflect one heart—God's faithful heart of love for His people warning them for their good.

And, that my friend, includes you.

You are loved and chosen and "not even death or life, angels or rulers, things present or things to come, hostile powers, height or depth, or any other created thing will have the power to separate us from the love of God" (Rom. 8:38-39).

Day 5
THE TRUE YOU

Call your brothers: My People
and your sisters: Compassion.
HOSEA 2:1

Now that you've read through Hosea and studied chapter 1, I'm curious about something. Can you relate to Gomer and Israel? Can you see your behavior in Israel's? Can you see Gomer's tendencies in your own? Probably. We are usually quick to see our weaknesses; quick to notice what we do wrong.

Let me put it this way, sister: I can see the "me" in Gomer and the "I" in Israel!

I've compared us to Gomer and Israel and called us chosen and loved several times this week so far, but—here is the big question—do you believe it? Do you believe you are chosen and loved by God? It's easy to look into the mirror that is our life and see why we shouldn't be chosen and loved—we're selfish, we wander from God, we have mixed motives, we aren't good enough … oh, the reasons we come up with!

The mirror of God's Word reflects the truth that we are chosen and loved. Before we can go on, you've gotta get this truth planted deep in your heart. Otherwise, you won't embrace the message of Hosea as God's message to you.

We'll finish up this week with just two truths: how you know you are chosen and how you know you are loved. Okey, dokey? And, from one sister to another, if you get nothing else out of this week of study—if you don't know who was king when Hosea was written, or which was the Northern and which was the Southern Kingdom—get these two truths. Stop right now and ask God to help you receive and believe these two truths about you.

1. YOU ARE CHOSEN.

Israel's story, Gomer's story, and your story are the same story. And at the core, it is a love story. But I haven't told you exactly why this is your story—why you, like Israel and Gomer, are chosen and loved.

You will love this!

HOSEA

Find Romans 9:24-26. Who is the "us" Paul is referring to?

The "us" is you and me, all of us who have received Christ as Savior.

Now, look at 1 Peter 2:10. What does Peter say about who we were and who we are now?

We were once not a people and now we are the people of God! Both Paul and Peter are talking about us, the church.

Paul referred to Hosea in that passage we read. Did you notice? He and Peter both pulled from a passage in Hosea that you are probably familiar with by now. It's Hosea 2:23.

Find it and mark the place because we will look at it last thing.

OK, stay with me. This will keep connecting you to Israel. Read Galatians 3:7-29. Focus on those last several verses, 26-29 because they pull this together. How does Paul describe you in those verses?

Fill in the blanks according to verse 29: If I belong to _____, I am one of _____ children and _____ according to the _____.

The reason you can read Hosea and see yourself in Israel is this: If you belong to Christ, you are Abraham's seed and you inherit all the promises he did!

Read what Jesus said about you in John 15:16. God chose you. You are chosen!

If you were one of those uncoordinated kids, like me, who was chosen last to be on a kick-ball team in PhysEd—and even then, you got chosen because there was no one left—you may need to rethink what it means to be chosen.

To be chosen by God means you are His first choice and His best choice. He didn't shrug His shoulders and say, "Well, I guess I'll take her if no one else will." No. When Jesus' hands were nailed to a cross, His fingers pointed to you—He chose to die for you. He chose you and He chooses you every day. Just like God chose Israel and Hosea chose Gomer, God chose you. You are a chosen woman of God.

2. YOU ARE LOVED.

It takes faith to trust that God chose you, doesn't it? When it comes to being chosen, we have to see ourselves in the mirror of our souls and state the truth, "God chose me." But when it comes to accepting that God loves us, we do something very different: we forget us.

We need to focus on God and His nature. His nature is love.

How does 1 John 4:8 describe God?

God is love. He is self-giving in His love because He is love. Nothing external provokes Him to love and nothing external prohibits His love. He is love. His love is a manifestation of His nature. When God is hurt, He bleeds love because He is love.

Since God is love, when do you think He started loving you?
☐ When I trusted Him as Savior
☐ When I cleaned up my act
☐ When I asked Him to forgive me of my sins
☐ He never started loving me

That was a trick question. Sorry! The answer may surprise you.

How does Jeremiah 31:3 describe the kind of love God loves you with?

God uses the word "everlasting" in describing His love. He says that He has loved us with an everlasting love.

When did "everlasting" begin? And when does it end?

God's love never started. Because He is eternal—self-existent—so is His love.

So, if He never started to love, He cannot cease to love.

God set His love upon you as He did upon Israel because He is love.

He doesn't love you because you are cleaned up, religious, or even because you are a Christian. He loves you because He is love. You didn't earn His love and you can't lose His love either. God didn't ring His hands, furrow His brow and analyze if you would qualify for His love. In many ways, He didn't make a decision to love you or not to love you—His essence is love, so for Him to know you is to love you. For Him to see you is to love you. He is love so He loves.

I know that is hard to grasp. But if you read 1 John 4:9-10, you see the ultimate proof of God's love for you.

God's love was revealed among us in this way: God sent His One and Only Son into the world so that we might live through Him. Love consists in this: not that we loved God, but that He loved us and sent His Son to be the propitiation for our sins.

1 JOHN 4:9-10

Jesus was the proof of God's love.

When you consider your lovability in light of God's loving nature and His proof of that love in Christ, you realize that you are loved because God is love. It is that simple, that deep, and that profound. That scandalous! You are loved because He is love.

Just because. That is why He loves you.

God's love is something you humbly accept by faith. For you to reject His love is to reject Him. To say you are not worthy of His love is to say He is not worthy of being love. To say you are not "good enough" is to say He is not good enough.

To reject that God's love applies to you is to reject the sacrifice of Christ and dismiss part of the character of God.

That means if we go back to that First Local Church of Hosea, crash their wedding, and watch Gomer walk down the aisle and think she is just not worthy of Hosea's love— that she was not, is not, and will never be the object of his love—if we reject Gomer's acceptability, we reject our own. If we can't accept that Gomer is chosen and loved, we probably won't accept that we are either.

When we cop the pose of low spiritual self-esteem, we are not only reducing our own worth, we are diminishing God. I know you don't mean to do that if you take on the not-me, not-good-enough excuse. That isn't my intention either, for sure. But essentially, that is what we are doing.

Think about it. You are God's beloved. That is your identity.

Can you just say this out loud? If someone is around, whisper it if you want. "I am loved because God is love." Good. Now say it again. "I am loved because God is love."

That is true my fellow Gomer. We are loved because God is love. We are the beloved. We are not the "be-tolerated," we are the "be-loved!"

Song of Solomon 7:10 reminds you that you are chosen and loved—you belong to your beloved and His desire is for you.

I belong to my love,
and his desire is for me.
SONG OF SONGS 7:10

Because you are God's beloved, you are living inside a love that is beyond you but still includes you.

God chose you. He loved you while you were still dirty. The Bible says, "while we were still sinners" (Rom. 5:8). He didn't choose to love you because you were lovely, He loved you and you became lovely. Your value comes from His inherit value.

Just like He chose to love Israel, He chooses to love you. Look into the mirror of your soul and see Gomer reflected back at you. She was the beloved bride and so are you. Can you embrace your true identity as a chosen and loved woman of God?

- Gomer's identity was not her past or her weakness, her identity was a chosen and loved bride.
- Israel's identity was not their good choices or bad choices; their identity was the loved and chosen people of God.
- Your identity is not your failure or past. Your identity is not your success or virtues. Your identity is not what you do, what you did, haven't done, should have done, or wished you'd done. Your identity is a chosen, loved woman whom God calls His beloved.

Can you begin to accept the you that God accepted?

Now, let's wind this up with the truth of Hosea 2:23 as God's word to you. God says to us who were not His people, "you are my people." And we will say back to Him, "You are my God!"

Way to make it through the first week of Hosea. He's starting to grow on you, isn't He? Now, sister, go be the beloved. Walk in the confidence that you are chosen and loved!

Group Session 2

BEFORE THE VIDEO
Welcome and Prayer

VIDEO NOTES: WHEN YOU SAY "I DO" TO I AM

When you said, "I do" to the I AM, you became the _____.

Because God is _____, you have _____.

Three Truths of My New Identity

    1. I am _____ _____ (Col. 3:12).

    2. I am _____ (Eph. 1:6).

    3. I am _____ (Col. 2:10).

CONVERSATION GUIDE
Video 2 and Week 1 Homework

DAY 1: What kinds of ideas do you think poetry can convey that prose cannot?

Discuss the idea of spiritual trifocals for understanding the Book of Hosea.

DAY 2: What adjectives come to mind to describe your first reading of the Book of Hosea?

What insights about Hosea did you pick up by reading The History of This Story? (p. 15) Do you see any parallels between culture today and in Hosea's day?

If Hosea's marriage to Gomer is a picture of God's relationship with Israel, what does that say about Hosea's marriage to Gomer? How do you think that relates to your marriage if you are married? (See Eph. 5:25-32.)

Why do you think Israel went after false gods and Gomer went for other lovers?

DAY 3: How do you respond to the idea that God could reach the end of His patience and actually become your enemy?

DAY 4: Why do you think God warns us so severely even though we are His beloved children?

DAY 5: What does the everlasting nature of God's love mean to you?

HOSEA

CONNECT WITH JENNIFER AT
JenniferRothschild.com/Hosea

He doesn't love you because you are cleaned up, religious, or even because you are a Christian. He loves you because He is love.
#HoseaStudy

WEEK TWO

OTHER LOVERS

HOSEA

Day 1
GOMERISMS:
WHY DID SHE DO IT?

Rebuke your mother; rebuke her.
For she is not My wife and I am not her husband.
Let her remove the promiscuous look from her face
and her adultery from between her breasts.
HOSEA 2:2

Hello, my fellow chosen and loved Gomer! This week we will tackle part of chapter 2. In fact, as soon as you finish reading this paragraph, turn to Hosea and read all of chapter 2. As you read it, remember Hosea is preaching to Israel about their idolatrous relationship to God. As you get the big picture of chapter 2, notice how the chapter falls into two parts: Rebuke is verses 2-13. Restoration is verses 14-21. OK, ready, set, read!

Done? Great.

Or, not so great? The chapter starts off pretty rough, doesn't it?

Hosea 2:2-4 gives a pretty ugly, graphic description of Israel's unfaithfulness. Hosea draws on the picture of an unfaithful wife to give this PG-13 rated account. But, Hosea is speaking of Israel here. Remember, though children are mentioned in verse 4, Hosea is using descriptive language to warn Israel that their behavior will have a ripple effect from generation to generation.

The take-away I want you to see is that both Israel and Gomer were bad deciders. We know by now that they didn't make good choices, but, I think we need to see why they made such bad decisions.

Since we, like Israel and Gomer, are capable of similar bad choices, why do you think we do what we do?

Think back to a really, really bad decision you made somewhere along the way. We all have them. They may look different, but we've all made our own versions. OK, do you have a situation in mind? Now what may seem to be a silly question: Why did you do it?

Out of fear, or stress, or selfishness, or shame, or any of a hundred reasons, we made a choice we really knew we shouldn't make. Once the ball started rolling the repercussions piled on. Somewhere along the line we look back and think, why in the world did I do that? Examining some of Israel's bad decisions helps us understand our own.

Because Hosea isn't written in a linear fashion, Israel's bad decisions are spread throughout the book.

So, to see what they were doing that caused such severe language from Hosea here in chapter 2, write next to each of the following references what the Israelites were up to:

Hosea 4:2

Hosea 4:12

Hosea 6:8

Hosea 8:4

Have you ever made any of those bad decisions? Circle above the answers that apply to you.

Now, look at what you did not circle. Chances are you didn't circle murder, or consulting a diviner's rod. Or, maybe there were just some things you didn't want anyone else to see. That's OK. And, you may not have circled things like idol worship or mixing with foreign nations because you think they don't apply to you. But, can you transfer those things from Hosea and Gomer's backyard to your own?

HOSEA

What could be our cultural equivalent to the following bad decisions?

1. Idol making and worship:

2. Consulting idols or diviners' rods:

3. Mixing with foreign nations:

4. Demanding your own king:

Sure, we don't spend much time at "Idols R Us" finding the perfect idol to consult. But it could be that your idol making and worship is in the form of creating gods out of things you own, or want, or people you admire. And, worshiping those idols would be your way of giving them lots of focus, credit, or power in your life.

Maybe consulting a divining rod would be like listening to superstition or even granting too much importance to your intuition or feelings over listening to God's truth. Bad decisions, right?

Then there's mixing with other nations. For the Israelites, God told them not to inter-marry because foreign nations worshiped idols and He didn't want them to get confused and unfaithful. Intermarriage for us means outside the faith (see 2 Cor. 6:14). Mixing with other nations could be represented in our culture by being caught up and mixed in with secular or worldly things or thinking; having a diluted or polluted form of faith.

Finally, demanding your own king. For Israel, God just gave them what they wanted; they were so sure they wanted a king—their own choice, their own way. It wasn't what God wanted for them, but He gave it to them anyway. Well, for you? Could demanding your own king be like demanding your own way? You being the boss of everything? Your way or no way?

Those things represent what I call "Gomerisms" and they put you on the wrong path. And a path is exactly where we will find Israel and Gomer in the next few days.

Let me just summarize what Gomerisms are. I put them into four categories for you.

Beside each of my descriptions of Gomerisms put a percentage. Just your honest estimate of how great a hold that Gomerism has in your life. I doubt that any of us are at 0% or 100% on any of them.

___% Trusting in my own wisdom is a Gomerism.

___% Misdirecting my worship is a Gomerism.

___% Elevating my wants is a Gomerism.

___% Demanding my way is a Gomerism.

Gomerisms are bad decisions! Think about those Gomerisms. Ask God if some of them are part of your life and why. Maybe you are like Gomer—you make some bad decisions because you haven't totally embraced that you are chosen and loved and so you seek love in the wrong ways and in the wrong places by demanding your way, and trusting your own wisdom over God's.

From one sister to another, let's really think hard about this. Do you deal with Gomerisms? You probably do; we all do. Jot down the ones you struggle with most and mention them to a Bible-study buddy. Pray with her and help each other choose one Gomerism to start working on. We Gomers need each other!

HOSEA

Day 2
THE AFFAIR

Yes, their mother is promiscuous;
She conceived them and acted shamefully.
For she thought, "I will go after my lovers,
the men who give me my food and water,
my wool and flax, my oil and drink."
HOSEA 2:5

So, now we arrive at the part of Hosea and Gomer's story you may not really relate to because you may think you've never acted as selfishly as Gomer did. Maybe you'd never leave your husband or children like she did. Or, your story might be similar to hers. I don't know, and that really isn't the point. The point is that we're all prone to wander. We all deal with Gomerisms.

In your own words, what did Gomer say in Hosea 2:5?

Gomer decided to go after her lovers. In other words, she had an affair; she went after other lovers, stepped out on Hosea, slept around. And, eventually, she left Hosea and her kids. Why? Gomer thought her lovers could give her something better than what Hosea gave her and that would make her feel something she wasn't feeling being stuck at home with just Hosea.

According to that verse, what did Gomer get from other lovers?

What might those three categories represent in your life? Here are my suggestions.
1. Bread and water represented daily needs being met. Survival starts with food, the most basic building block of security.

What is your bread and water? What makes you feel secure? Or what do you think you can't do without?

2. Women in Gomer's day used wool and flax to make fabric. You know, clothes! Perhaps wool and flax could represent your wardrobe, thus your appearance, the physical impression you make on others.

What would you say represents your wool and flax?

3. Oil and drink were the pleasure commodities of Gomer's day. The sweetness of the grape was a delight to the soul and pleasure to the taste.

What is your oil and wine? What is your 'go to' for pleasure?

Now, look at what you wrote and let me ask you this: Is anything wrong with bread and water, wool and flax, or oil and wine? Is anything wrong with desiring your basic needs for food and shelter to be met? Is anything wrong with wanting to make a good impression, have nice clothes, or look good? And is anything wrong in desiring pleasure—enjoying nice food or drink, traveling, decorating, or whatever else brings you happiness?

No way. All those are good things. Yahweh only gives good things. It's normal and healthy to desire those good things in their proper place under the lordship of Christ.

I'm sure Hosea gave Gomer shelter and security, clothes and good things that brought her pleasure. But Gomer wanted what she didn't have, not what she did have. The grass seemed greener on the other side of her fence.

I can relate; can't you? I could be perfectly happy, then I learn about the latest cell phone case or trendy handbag or something someone else has that I don't. Suddenly my happiness dissolves and I can easily begin to think, *I've got to have one of those to be happy.*

Why do you suppose something in us can make our happiness seem dependent on having what others have?

Think about what motivates you. Where do you find your buzz or sense of identity? Check any that seem to apply.

☐ relationships   ☐ my career

☐ food   ☐ my kids

☐ shopping   ☐ money

☐ my appearance   ☐ being morally good and admired

☐ approval of others

The things you marked, are they instead of God or along with God? Really think about that. Beside each answer you chose, put an "I" for "instead of" or an "A" for "also."

It may be hard for you to know your answer because this is the first time you've thought about this. If so, linger as long as you need until you get some clarity. Ask God; His Spirit will show you. The reason this matters is that what starts as "also" usually becomes "instead of." I will come back to this later. But, if you want to see what I mean, read Hosea 8:11.

Gomer had her needs met in Hosea. She could have had many of her desires fulfilled within her marriage. But she looked outside of Hosea to get her needs and wants fulfilled. She wanted something more.

We can't know just what motivated Gomer, but I think it is very possible that Gomer never identified with who she was in her marriage covenant. So she went outside her marriage to find her identity.

Once she said "I do," she was no longer Gomer the harlot; she was Gomer the bride, the beloved wife. But, she didn't identify with her new and true identity; she went outside of her covenant to find her status and sense of self.

Put simply, she didn't act out of her identity; she acted out of her Iddiction.

Iddiction... that word is not a typo. Let me explain.

If you are Gomeristic at all, then you are probably an Iddict too. An Iddict is someone who is addicted to herself—her wants, her wisdom, her whims, her way. And if you are an Iddict, it is because you are trying to find your identity in yourself—Iddiction; in following your whims, trusting your wisdom, elevating your wants, and getting your way. When we go to food or shopping to satisfy our esteem needs; when we find our sense of self in our career, appearance, or the impression we make on others; when our kids' behavior, our homes, or our successes make us feel like somebody, it's because we haven't identified fully with our identity in God and, therefore, we act out of our Iddiction rather than our identity.

Gomer tried to find her identity in herself and her lovers because she never identified with her new identity as a chosen, loved woman.

If you were Gomer's tennis partner, fellow scrapbooker, or walking buddy, and you were about to hang out with her, what would you tell her about herself that she may be overlooking?

Do you need to say those same words to yourself?

You too are a chosen, loved woman. Do you identify with your identity?

OK, pause here. What do you think about that? Does that make sense to you? Take a long look into the mirror of your soul. Does the woman reflected back at you find her identity in God, in the truth that she is chosen and loved? Or, does that woman who looks back at you look more like an Iddict trying to find herself and her identity in other places and people?

I just want you to begin pondering this. Journal your thoughts.

HOSEA

The verses below may help you identify how Iddicted you are. Israel, like Gomer, had Identity but they acted out of their Iddiction. Look in these verses and see what I mean:

	IDENTITY	IDDICTION
ISRAEL	Deuteronomy 7:6 *God's chosen people*	Hosea 4:16-17 *Obstinate and stubborn*
GOMER	Hosea 2:19; 3:3 *Hosea's beloved,* *faithful to her*	Hosea 2:5 *Prefers other lovers*
US	1 Peter 2:9 *Chosen and royal*	2 Timothy 3:4-5 *A form of godliness with no power* Matthew 15:13 *Draw near with lips but hearts are far from God*

Oh, my fellow Gomer, we must begin to identify with our identity in Christ. When we don't, Gomerisms get the best of us and we follow "my way, my whims, my wisdom." In other words, our wandering hearts lead us straight to ourselves ... the dead end of me! We fall into Iddiction.

I have recognized and admit that I am an Iddict—a recovering Iddict! Are you?

Today, ask God to reveal if you are. Or, may I say, how much of an Iddict you are, because we all struggle with Iddiction.

I think we should all show up to our next Bible study and take turns saying, "Hi, I'm Jennifer, and I am a recovering Iddict, but I am choosing God over Gomerisms!"

Can I get an Amen? Amen!

Day 3
THE INTERVENTION

Therefore, this is what I will do:
I will block her way with thorns;
I will enclose her with a wall,
So that she cannot find her paths.
HOSEA 2:6

Hey, Gomer Girl! We talked yesterday about our Iddiction. When we love someone who has an addiction sometimes only an intervention will do. Well, the same applies to our Iddiction. Sometimes, we too need an intervention. God did that for Israel; He performed an Iddict-tervention.

How did God intervene according to Hosea 2:6?

He will block their way with thorns, enclose them with a wall, and obscure their paths. God is saying there will be a bad result to a bad decision. A dead end.

Have you ever gotten caught up in thorns? You can pass through eventually, but it sure slows you down, cuts you up, and makes you think twice, doesn't it? God is saying He will block Gomer's/Israel's wayward way with thorns.

Can you think of any "thorns" that God may have put in your path to slow you down and make you think twice about something you were doing?

How about a wall? Have you ever experienced a wall from God that blocked your way—forget slowing down and thinking twice, you just had to stop right where you were?

Thorns and walls are never pleasant, but they remind us that God loves us—loves us enough to slow us down and draw us back to Himself.

Thankfully, God is not an enabler of our Iddictive behavior. He loves us too much! God sometimes provides a barrier opposing our way. Out of protection and love for us, He plants thorns in the avenue and our turnpike becomes a turn-around!

Those thorns and walls are like the hands of God pushing against you; resisting you.

If you look in the New Testament, both James and Peter quote Proverbs 3:34 and it tells us who God resists. Who is it?

"God resists the proud, but gives grace to the humble"
JAMES 4:6, 1 PETER 5:5

Think about the thorny roadblocks you noted. Did humility lead you to that place? I doubt it! At least for me, humility never steers me wrong but pride is never a good GPS—I always end up in a mess when I follow its path.

God will resist pride in us because He loves us. If He resists you because of your own pride, don't misunderstand and think God is rejecting you. It's actually the opposite. He resists you in order to receive you back to Himself. When you finally get tired of being tangled up in the thorns of your way, your wisdom, and your wants, you will turn back to Him in humility. Then, God gives you the grace to get untangled and turn back to Him.

How do you usually respond when you feel God's resistance?

Angry   Frustrated   Deflated

Grateful   Confused   Unloved   Rejected

God blocking our efforts may feel negative, but that's not necessarily the case.

Find Psalm 119:67 and 71. Rephrase the psalmist's words so they apply to something you have gone through, or are going through; you know, thorns or walls.

What the psalmist calls "affliction" we could call "trials" or a million other things that go wrong in our lives. God can use affliction as a form of loving resistance to keep us from going astray or to guide us back to His Word. Sister, don't resent God if He resists you. Often, what feels like resistance is an affirmation that you belong to God.

Find Proverbs 13:24 and Hebrews 12:6. What is the basic point made in both those passages?

A loving parent disciplines her child because she loves him. She resists him when he is heading down the wrong path; she doesn't let him run wild.

Our loving Father God sometimes stops us in our tracks when our Gomeristic path of Iddiction is leading us to choices, places, or people that will bring us harm or pain.

Remember the Bible promise that says "all things work together for the good of those who love God" (Rom. 8:28)? Well, roadblocks, afflictions, thorns and walls are all part of the "things" that God uses for our good.

But the reason God lovingly tangles us in thorns is ultimately found in Romans 8:29 He has committed to conform those who belong to Him to the image of His Son. If you belong to Christ, God has a personal commitment to keep you on His path, with Him— even if that means He will let you bang into a wall or get tangled in thorns to get you back on track.

Now, let's go on to Hosea 2:7. This verse opens an entirely different issue from Gomer's perspective. And you may really relate to it.

> She will pursue her lovers but not catch them;
> She will seek them but not find them.
> Then she will think,
> "I will go back to my former husband,
> For then it was better for me than now."
> HOSEA 2:7

What does Hosea 2:7 say about Gomer's success rate with her lovers?

Gomer and Israel not only faced obstacles placed there by God. They also ran upon a basic reality of human experience that we all can relate to. Philosophers have called it the paradox of hedonism. Ever heard of it? If not, once you read what it is, you'll identify by firsthand experience—I bet you've lived it. I certainly have.

The paradox says the harder you try to find happiness the further from you it goes. William Bennett expressed it this way: "Happiness is like a cat, if you try to coax it or call it, it will avoid you; it will never come. But if you pay no attention to it and go about your business, you'll find it rubbing against your legs and jumping into your lap."[1] That's a purr-fect example, isn't it? (I know, silly. I couldn't resist!)

> They will eat but not be satisfied;
> They will be promiscuous but not multiply.
> For they have abandoned their devotion to the LORD.
> HOSEA 4:10

How does Hosea 4:10 reflect the paradox of hedonism?

The end result of our Iddiction is not satisfaction; it's an empty, unhappy identity crisis. A life of pursuing pleasure doesn't bring happiness, it brings exhaustion.

1. William Bennett, as quoted by Michael Horton, *Ordinary* (Grand Rapids, MI: Zondervan, 2014), 57-58.

For Gomer, this meant she went after human lovers and wound up wounded and enslaved. For Israel, this meant they went after other gods they believed offered power and prosperity. They wound up leaderless, defenseless, and ultimately destroyed.

When you see that result, doesn't it make you grateful that God lovingly blocks our paths? Oh Lord, bring on the roadblocks!

As we finish up, read the words of David.

The boundary lines have fallen for me in pleasant places;
I have a beautiful inheritance.
PSALM 16:6

Just think about the boundaries God has set for your life. In what sense are those boundaries pleasant?

God has lovingly placed us within the boundary of His covenant, the best path for us—a path with boundaries that are pleasant, not restrictive. That boundary is a pleasant place, a place of identity, security, and wholeness. We do have a delightful inheritance of satisfaction, peace, and purpose.

So, Gomer Girl, if you've been tangled in thorns, or banging your head against the wall God lovingly erected, turn around and go back to your first and best love—God, the Lover of your soul.

HOSEA

Day 4
GIVE CREDIT WHERE CREDIT IS DUE

> She does not recognize
> that it is I who gave her the grain,
> the new wine, and the oil.
> I lavished silver and gold on her,
> which they used for Baal.
> **HOSEA 2:8**

Today we're going to start with some culture! So go put on your best black dress and let's catch a cab to Carnegie Hall. Yep, you and I are going to attend a Yo-Yo Ma concert because we're so uptown. Turn off your cell phone because this will be like nothing you've ever heard. The master cellist begins to play. It's a Brahms recital. You are moved. The crowd is touched. The concert hall is hushed. Finally upon the last note, the audience bursts forth in applause. You can barely stay in your seat and keep from hollering. "Bravo, bravo," they cry. "Bravo, bravo for the cello!"

For the cello? Huh? You don't go to many concerts at Carnegie Hall, but that just doesn't seem right to you, does it?

That would never happen, would it? It happens all the time. Not in concert halls. Audiences are keen enough to give honor to the master, to the player, not to the musical gift he offers. But, in real life, we misplace honor every day. And so did Gomer and Israel. That was what God was pointing out in this section of Hosea. Hosea 2:8 demonstrates what I mean. Our girl Gomer didn't recognize that what she had was from Hosea.

Gomer had made it clear that she went after her lovers because they gave her all the good stuff—like wool and flax, oil and wine, and bread and water—remember?

Not only did Gomer not honor the giver, she dishonored the giver by giving that good stuff, or giving credit for that good stuff, to her lovers.

Likewise, Israel didn't recognize that what they had, they got from God. Israel did not honor God for His gifts. Instead, they honored idols with the gifts God gave them.

We often do the same. We don't recognize that all the good we have comes from God.

We're so prone to wander that we take credit for what God gives us.
For example, from whom did Israel say their riches came? (Hosea 12:8)

See what I mean? God gave Israel riches. Israel took credit for getting those riches all by themselves. Think about what you have—talents, appearance, success, family, security… do you take credit for those things in your life?

Now, I know you're tempted to shout out a "no way!" But, I don't want you to answer that question with words, I want you to look at your life and see how your lifestyle and attitude are answering that question in your most unguarded moments on any ordinary day. Just think about that.

We often live in a way that we take credit for who we are, what we have, and what we can do. How could that show up in your life?

Now, sometimes we don't take credit from God and give it to ourselves; sometimes we take credit from God and put it somewhere else entirely.

What did Gomer say came from her lovers? (Hosea 2:12)

Vines and fig trees from her lovers? Really? Did they create the seed and grow the vine and tree? How ludicrous to give man credit for what only God can do. But we do this when we enjoy what God gives us without acknowledging the God who gives them to us.

Vines and fig trees in the Old Testament often represent tranquility, security, and enjoyment of property. They also represent fruitfulness. Put simply, the vines and fig trees speak of safety, pleasure, and peace. Gomer/Israel credits her lovers with her sense of safety, pleasure, and peace. So I ask the hard question: Does safety, pleasure, and peace originate from any source other than God? Can you really experience peace, pleasure, and safety outside of God?

Only the true God gives true security. Only the Holy God gives pure pleasure and only the unchanging God can provide unshakable peace.

A false god can only offer you a false sense of security, a temporary lack of conflict you confuse with peace, and fleeting elation you think is pleasure until it fizzles out.

What are your vines and fig trees? What is, or are, the things in your life that you associate with safety, peace, and pleasure?

Because they are from the divine gift Giver, it's not much of a stretch for us to forget the Giver and simply fixate on the gift. That is part of being an Iddict who is prone to wander.

Now read Hosea 2:9-12 and notice how God will react to this misplaced honor. In one or two words, describe the action He will take.

God was taking it back.

Since Gomer (and Israel) had abandoned Him, Yahweh took away the blessings He had given. Those fig trees and vines represented their fruitfulness. All of these things belong to God. He can do with them whatever He wishes.

How would you feel if God "repossessed" your fig tree and vines?
□ nervous   □ relieved
□ uncomfortable   □ humbled
□ insecure   □ angry

Your response to that question reveals the degree to which your identity and sense of security is found in things from God rather than in God Himself.

When I wrote that sentence, I thought how much I need to meditate about that and I bet you do too. So I will turn it into a question that we can pray about and ask God to help us answer honestly: Is my sense of security and identity in God alone, or do I find my identity and sense of security in things from God—like my talents, success, kids, appearance, and blessings?

How secure would I feel if I lost those things? Who would I be if I didn't have those things to identify me?

Lord, guide us into truth. We want to find our identity and security in You—You alone. Amen.

Day 5
THE DEMAND OF OTHER LOVERS

And I will punish her for the days of the Baals
when she burned incense to them,
put on her rings and jewelry,
and went after her lovers,
but forgot Me.
HOSEA 2:13

Well, we are going to finish up this last half of chapter 2 and I will be glad to get to the restoration. How about you? Oh girl, the second half of this chapter is one of my favorite parts of Hosea, so get ready. But, today, let's put the last nail in this coffin and bury this dark part of Hosea, OK? In Hosea 2:13 Israel was worshiping Baal—a false god, an idol. And, remember, in Hosea, Gomer's lovers and Israel's idols are the same things.

What are the three things that Gomer/Israel did when it came to their "lovers"?
1.
2.
3.

She burnt incense, put on her bling, and went after her lovers. But, how does the last phrase of that verse summarize her actions?

She forgot God. That's what happens when any of us go for other lovers of pleasure, acceptance, or status. We forget the true Lover of our souls and look for love for our souls in all the wrong places. That's what Israel was doing by worshiping Baal. They were trying to get satisfaction from a source other than the true God.

Israel worshiped Baal—the Canaanite god of rain and fertility—their idol, along with their worship of the one true God. Part of Baal worship included engaging with temple prostitutes. So, you can see why Hosea is often rated PG-13.

HOSEA

Read Hosea 4:1-3 to get a sad summary of the condition of Israel while they worshiped Baal. Now skip down to Hosea 4:7 to see what Israel did by worshiping idols; what Gomer did by leaving Hosea for other lovers; and what we do when we stray from God to find our identity or satisfaction in other things or people.

What do we exchange? (Hosea 4:7) We exchange _____ for _____.

We exchange our glorious God for something disgraceful. Israel did that by mixing worship for Yahweh with worship for Baal.

That is exactly what happened to our Gomer Girl too! She exchanged her marriage for an affair, love for lust, her husband for a lover, her identity as a beloved bride for the indignity of a prostitute. And the result of her choice shows up in chapter 3. I know, I know, we aren't even done with chapter 2 but, you just need to jump to chapter 3 anyway.

Go ahead and read Hosea 3:1. Check what best represents what happened to Gomer.
□ Gomer needed to be bailed out of jail.
□ Gomer was stuck in a traveling circus.
□ Gomer needed to be purchased from slavery.
□ Gomer needed help moving out of her latest lover's home.

Gomer exchanged her freedom for slavery. She was stuck.

The cost of other lovers is steep. Iddiction can lead to idolatry and idolatry leads to slavery. Smarter brains than mine who studied this think that Gomer could have wound up married to another man, in a common law kind of way. And because she was "property," he was putting her up for sale. That way, another man could pay the debt she had created. Or Gomer could have become a prostitute and the pimp who had "employed" her could have been looking to get as much out of her and, for her, as possible. During this period in Israel, many women were actually temple prostitutes, either by choice or necessity, and that could have also been Gomer's situation. We don't know for sure. But we do know that she was no longer free. The party ended. She went from glorious to disgraced. As God said of Israel, they "became as vile as the thing they loved" (Hosea 9:10, NIV).

Gomer ended up at a slave auction because she was to be sold. It is as if she went from the latest headline to yesterday's news; from Chanel to chains; from Prada to prostitution; from the beloved bride to the overlooked and discarded.

To leave God for other lovers of self or sin is costly. We find ourselves stuck and ashamed. Look at how Hosea described Israel. It sounds a lot like where Gomer ended up, and me and you when we are stuck in sin.

Israel is swallowed up;
now she is among the nations
like something no one wants.
For they have gone up to Assyria
like a wild donkey wandering alone.
Ephraim has sold herself to lovers.
HOSEA 8:8-9, NIV

Do you ever feel like Gomer or Israel? Describe times you have felt ...

swallowed up:

wandering alone:

like something no one wanted:

Those aren't good feelings, are they? But, those hard emotions are what Gomerisms and Iddiction leave us with. And, when we feel those feelings, we can feel desperate and stuck. But, Gomer Girl, if you feel those feelings, you are not alone and you are not stuck. If you feel stuck on a slave block of your own making, do not get address labels made because the slave block is not your permanent address!

Though Scripture describes Gomer and Israel as "swallowed up," "wandering alone," "like something no one wanted," and said she had "sold herself," God still wanted her—His love never wavered. He said,

I will heal their waywardness and love them freely,
for my anger has turned away from them.
HOSEA 14:4, NIV

You may want to feel the chains for a while. Sit before the Lord, the Lover of your soul, and let Him show you where you are stuck so you will be ready for the buy back! Redemption is on its way. And all the sisters say ... "Amen!"

Group Session 3

BEFORE THE VIDEO
Welcome and Prayer

VIDEO NOTES
When You Ain't Got Yada, You Ain't Got Nada

When we wander from God, usually our problem is a lack of _____.

When we see the word *know* in the Book of Hosea, it is usually the Hebrew word *yada* which means "an _____ knowing."

When we stray from God, we stray from our sense of self because we don't *yada* our _____ of self.

Sarah did not _____ herself because she did not *yada* God.

Naomi's grandson, Obed, grew up to become the father of Jesse and Jesse the father of _____. And Jesus Christ came from the _____ of David.

In the Book of Hosea, "knowledge of God" is *daath Elohim* in Hebrew and shows an empathetic _____ to God.

Revelation 2:5 gives us the following steps to *yada*:

1. Consider from where you have _____.

2. _____.

3. Do the things you did at _____.

God doesn't want us to sacrifice _____ with Him for activity for Him.

CONVERSATION GUIDE
Video 3 and Week 2 Homework

DAY 1: Why do you think we are so capable of such bad decisions?

What cultural equivalents do you think describe our versions of: making and worshiping idols, consulting idols or diviners' rods, mixing with foreign nations, or demanding our own king?

DAY 2: Why do you suppose something in us can make our happiness seem dependent on having what others have?

How do you think we can tell when something begins to move from an "also" to an "instead of" God?

If you had the chance, what would you warn Gomer that she may be overlooking?

DAY 3: Would you want to share any thorns God has set in your path in the past to intervene in a direction you were going?

How does Hosea 4:10 reflect the paradox of hedonism?

In what sense can you identify with David that the boundaries God has set for your life are pleasant?

DAY 4: What is, or are, the things in your life that you associate with safety, peace, and pleasure? How do you react when they are taken away?

DAY 5: What kinds of situations tempt you to feel: swallowed up? Wandering alone? Like something no one wanted?

HOSEA

CONNECT WITH JENNIFER AT
JenniferRothschild.com/Hosea

Gomer tried to find identity in herself and lovers because she never
identified with her new identity as a chosen, loved woman.
#HoseaStudy

WEEK THREE

LOVED AGAIN

HOSEA

Day 1
THE BUY BACK

> Then the LORD said to me, "Go again; show love to a woman who is loved by another man and is an adulteress, just as the LORD loves the Israelites though they turn to other gods and love raisin cakes."
> HOSEA 3:1

Hey, you loved, accepted, and complete woman of God! You, Gomer Girl, are the beloved!

This week we are going to experience incredible forgiveness and restoration. So, let's go back to the slave block where we left Gomer, hopeless and alone. That is a terrible way to leave a friend, isn't it? And I feel like Gomer is a friend. Do you? Even though we left her alone on the slave block, she was not forgotten. While Gomer was feeling unloved, God and Hosea had something totally radical in mind.

Look at Hosea 3:1 again. What did God tell Hosea to show? _____

Notice what God did not tell Hosea to do. God didn't say, "Go show judgment" or "Go show disdain to your wife." God told Hosea to show love. Love! Gomer had not only been loved by "another" (that may have been a ginormous understatement), she had likely been loved by many others.

We've been trying to identify with Gomer, but shift for a second. How would you feel if you were Hosea, asked to do such a thing?

He must have felt betrayed, like it wasn't fair, or right, that he should have to do such a thing. It had to be incredibly humbling.

At that moment, maybe Hosea needed to love God more than he loved Gomer in order to obey. We can't forget that Hosea was not super-husband. He was human-husband. He had to feel hurt by Gomer. He probably fought feelings of disgust. He was certainly humiliated in front of the men in town. He was a spiritual leader in the community and his wife had left him and committed flat-out, in-your-face adultery, over, and over.

We cannot overestimate what this must have been like for him and how he must have felt. But he was called by God and he followed God. I can only imagine that His willingness to obey gave him the strength to obey. And deep down, don't you hope he still loved her? Missed her? Either way, it took sheer humility and strength to go get her back.

But he went.

According to Hosea 3:2, what was the payment he gave for her?

He paid 15 shekels of silver, a homer of barley, and a lethech of barley (ESV). Well, I don't know about you, but that was totally meaningless to me. I had no idea what value that represented in their time. So I looked it up.

In verse 2 the use of the word *lethech* is a *hapax legomenon*. What? You don't know what that is? Ha! I sure didn't. *Hapax legomenon* means *a word which occurs only once in a document*. *Lethech* appears in the Old Testament only here in Hosea 3:2.

Because of this unique use of the word in Hosea, the versions differ on the translation of verse 2. Some translators assume that the *lethech* is a half of a homer. Yeah, that means a lot to you, I know. So here's the straight scoop on a homer. It was a unit of dry measure, estimated between 3.8 and 6.6 bushels. Others assume that the homer and the *lethech* are different terms for dry measures, but, that too, makes me scratch my head and say, "huh?" Some versions even render that word as a skin of wine. After reading all of the educated guesses, I have to go with the idea that the *lethech* was likely a half a homer.

Likely, a homer and a half of barley was worth about 15 pieces of silver. So if you do the math, Gomer has a price tag on her of 30 pieces of silver. So picture it—15 pieces of silver and a big ole bag of barley along with a not-so-big bag of barley. That's what it cost Hosea to get Gomer back. Next let's try to get a grip on how valuable Gomer was.

According to Exodus 21:32, what was valued at 30 pieces of silver?

Gomer was equal in value to a slave according to the law of the goring ox in Exodus. Now, look at Leviticus 27:2-4. What else was valued at 30 shekels of silver?

In Leviticus 27:2, the NIV renders the idea of making a vow to dedicate someone to the Lord. If you were dedicating a woman, you were to be assessed 30 pieces of silver. The

NASB translation reads when you make a "difficult vow" you are to be charged based on the value of the person. It's kind of like how an insurance company would pay more for an injury based on time lost from work.

> So put yourself on the slave block with Gomer. How much would you hope someone would pay for you if that price suggested your value?
>
> What does the truth of 1 Peter 1:18-19 suggest about your value?

You were worth the life of Jesus. That is how valuable you are to Him. You may not feel that special or valuable, but, Gomer Girl, who you are and how you feel are not the same thing. Trust God's opinion of you. He sees you as incredibly, eternally, valuable.

> What are your thoughts? Formulate them into a prayer of thanks to God, or a prayer of petition asking God to help you internalize the truth of your value.

Back to the slave block. Hosea paid 30 pieces of silver for Gomer—the price of a slave. What if you were purchased with the cost of a slave? How would you expect to be treated?

I would expect to be a lifelong slave of the one who bought me.

When Hosea spoke to Gomer after redeeming her, he didn't say, "Come home and serve me. Be my slave." He could have, right? After all, he just bought her for the price of a slave.

But Hosea 3:3 doesn't give that impression.

> What does Hosea invite Gomer to do in Hosea 3:3?

He asks her to live with him as his wife in faithfulness. He tells her there will be a short time of probation and he will be faithful to her too. But he does not say that her role is forever altered. No more wife, now just the house keeper. No more wife, now just the concubine. The beauty of her redemption is that it includes restoration.

So does your redemption. It includes restoration.

What was lost in the garden was redeemed on the cross. What sin destroyed in Eden, God restored through Calvary!

> Oh sister! I feel a verse coming on! You need to find 2 Corinthians 5:17, change the word "he" to "she" and read it out loud now. Right now. Yes, now! Louder!

If you are in Christ, my fellow Gomer, old things are passed away and behold! That means, stop and notice! Behold, *poof!* All, not just some, but all, all things are made new! Redeemed and restored! Thank You, Jesus!

God does not redeem without restoring. Even Israel will be restored to the bride again. Eugene Peterson paraphrases God's restorative words to Israel this way: "Never again will you address me, 'My slave-master!'" (Hosea 2:16 MSG).

When God redeems us—even though we may feel like we have no valuable position in His heart; even though we may feel like a slave—God expects us to treat Him not as slave-master but as husband. That means we must receive our identity as the loved, accepted bride and act like it. We must trust in His love and forgiveness.

Finally, for today, I want you to think about 30 pieces of silver. That phrase sounds familiar doesn't it?

> What New Testament reference to "30 pieces of silver" comes to mind? If you want to check, look to Matthew 26:15. Who was also sold for that price?

> How does it make you feel that Jesus allowed Himself to be sold for the price of a slave? How does it make you feel that Jesus specifically connected His value to that of a woman? Write your feelings to Him.

Oh Gomer Girl, He made Himself nothing so we could be somebody. His beautiful life gives our lives beauty. Let's honor Him with our humility and gratefulness today. Amen!

HOSEA

Day 2
GOD'S SHOCKING RESPONSE

Therefore, I am going to persuade her,
lead her to the wilderness,
and speak tenderly to her.
HOSEA 2:14

Let's summarize where we are in Hosea. Both Israel and Gomer have followed crooked paths straight into trouble! They have chased after other lovers. They have betrayed the one who loved them most.

We can't fully identify with how God must have felt, but, have you ever felt betrayed? How did you feel?

Betrayal makes me feel unimportant, hurt, dishonored, and angry. When I have felt betrayed, I want to run as far from that person as possible and never trust them again. In my not-so-Christlike moments, I want them to feel as awful as they made me feel. Punish the rascal!

I'm an imperfect woman, and my response is imperfect too.
But, how would you expect a perfect God to respond?
□ destroy them
□ remove His blessing from them
□ ignore them
□ punish them
□ other

God has every right to rebuke and destroy. If you want to see what
I mean, read Hosea 10:2.

God would be just in His actions if He destroyed them down to the subatomic level. But He doesn't. Instead of speaking harshly, the long-suffering God of Israel speaks tenderly to His people.

Is that not almost too much to bear? Just when you think God is done, He does not treat any of us as our sins deserve. In fact, he shows us kindness.

Look at Romans 2:4 and jot down the result of God's kindness.

I will go back to my former husband,
for then it was better for me than now.
HOSEA 2:7

What does Hosea 2:7 reveal about God's hopeful expectation?

God treats His people kindly and holds out hope that Israel will repent and return to the truth that God alone is the perfect Lover of their souls.

But look at Hosea 2:15. God wants us to return because He wants to bless us.

Fill in the blanks to reveal the blessing.

There I will _____and
make the Valley of Achor into a _____of_____.

God's going to make her valley of trouble into a door of hope! Have you heard of the Valley of Achor?

When the Israelites, under the leadership of Joshua, entered the promised land, one of the first places they came upon was a valley near Jericho. The valley was called Achor. The word *Achor* means *muddy*, or *turbid*. The name may be connected to the rolling waters of the Jordan at flood stage. So here's how to view the Valley of Achor:

1. THE EARLY DAYS

When Israelite grandmas were kneading dough and talking about the good old days when they first lived in their homeland, they would have thought of Achor. It would be like the early days in some phase of your life. Maybe it was when you moved into your first apartment, or when you went away to college. If you've been married a while, you can think of some images that represent being newlywed, right? I still have my first $35 wedding band that Phil gave me when I said "I do." It was all we could afford and when I think of our early days, I think of that ring. You know, like that ugly green couch you got at a garage sale. Or, perhaps the image that comes to mind when you think of your freshman year of college are the stuffed peppers that were served every Thursday in the cafeteria.

Those images would be like the Israelites remembrance of the churning Jordan at flood stage. Think of it like nostalgia—fond memories even if everything wasn't always perfect. These are the sweet memories that conjure up remembrances of the early days—the good old days.

> **What image comes to your mind when you think of the early days of some special phase of life for you?**

My $35 wedding band and what you wrote above are the sweet images of your Valley of Achor. But it isn't always sweet memories associated with the early days; sometimes it's bittersweet to remember your own "Valley of Achor."

2. THE HARD DAYS

The Valley of Achor was also bittersweet to the Israelites. Look at Joshua 7 if you need to recount how Israel conquered Jericho. It was a big city—a big victory. They had sweet memories of their first steps into the promised land. Then, they attacked Ai. It was a little city, but a big loss. This was a bitter memory for Israel because Achan's disobedience was the reason they lost to Ai. Achan and his family were then stoned—in the Valley of Achor. So, the image of Achor not only evoked the early days for Israel, but also a particular time of defeat and shame.

Do you have some Valley of Achor memories that are painful to think about? The wonderful times can also host the worst times. When I think of early days of my marriage,

I can't help but think of that cheap wedding band and smile. But I can also think of some ugly fights Phil and I had as newlyweds trying to adjust to married life—those Achor moments don't make me smile at all.

Get the point of Achor? Taken together, I think the Valley of Achor represented promise followed by problems. Triumph followed by trouble.

It's the human story, isn't it? Sterling silver shines and then tarnishes. Gomer says, "I do" and then says, "What have I done?" We walk in faith and then we wander off into unfaithfulness.

You can even see this in our American story. The early days of JFK's presidency were like Camelot, but it quickly turned into Achor when he was assassinated. Make sense?

Wayward Israel, and hopeless Gomer, would have heard this and it was as if God was saying, "I'll take the lowest point in your life, the time of spoiled potential, dashed hopes, and greatest shame, and I'll turn that into a honeymoon of new beginnings."

Wow. What a God!

Do you need God to turn your Valley of Achor into a door of hope? Oh Gomer Girl, He can and He wants to.

Write a prayer asking Him to open that door of hope … To be the door of hope you need.

Dear God,

Amen

We Gomer Girls need each other. Find a Bible Study buddy you can invite into your Valley of Achor. She can help that valley of trouble become a door of hope as she shines the light of Jesus over painful memories.

Jesus Himself is your Door of Hope, Sweet Gomer Girl. He loves, accepts, and completes you. So walk in His rest and restoration today.

Day 3
BACK TO THE DAYS
OF OUR YOUTH

There she will sing as in the days of her youth,
as in the day she came up out of Egypt.
HOSEA 2:15B (NIV)

I tell you, sister, the older I get, the more forgetful I get! Can I get a witness? Well, I found out why. When you and I were born, we came with all the brain cells we will ever get. That's why when you were a newborn, your head was one-quarter of your total length at birth. All those valuable brain cells don't regenerate once they're gone. So once those sweet little cells are damaged, they are not replaced. That is why your brain is reduced to only one-eighth of your total length by the time you reach adulthood. Sometimes I would love to have my brain restored to the proportion it was when I was in diapers!

> Look at the second half of Hosea 2:15 and jot down what God promises about Israel's youth.

> If your brain cells are behaving today, think about your youth. What was the very best part of youth for you?

One of Israel's best memories had to be when God delivered them from slavery in Egypt. I imagine they came out singing. But, shortly after, they were singing the blues, wandering in wilderness, disobeying God, losing battles, and worshiping idols. Sour notes for sure.

God is saying, "I am not only going to redeem you now, but my redemptive touch will not be confined to the present or even to the future." God's work in our lives renews everything that has come before—our best days and our worst days.

Let's visit another prophet, Joel, to see how this redemption and renewal works. He used a locust plague in the same way Hosea used his marriage as a sermon illustration. (Not to suggest a marriage partner and locusts have anything in common. Wink!)

What does Joel 2:25 promise to the ancient Israelites?

Just as none of us are as young as we once were, all of us have places in our lives where the "locusts" have eaten—hopes dashed, mistakes made, and losses piled on. God says He will repay all that damage.

> What do you think God means when He says He will repay? (Attention Type A: there is no right answer; I just want you to think about this)

The word *repay* in Joel 2:25 is *shalam*. Sound familiar? What word comes to mind when you see *shalam?* I bet you'd say *peace*. Me too; that's what comes to mind. But this word *shalam* means "to be safe (in mind, body or estate); figuratively, to be (causatively, make) completed."

Since Joel was talking about damage done in the past, he promised two things. God will make us safe from past damage, and He will make it somehow complete.

When Gomer said "I do" to Hosea, she became the beloved bride—complete. Her past was overwritten by her present. And, then, when she strayed and became enslaved, Hosea redeemed her and made her safe—even from past damage.

The idea that God completes our past, helps me understand Romans 8:28 even better. It says God makes all things work for the good of those who love Him, right?

> How does Joel's promise to make past damage both safe and complete add to your understanding or appreciation of Romans 8:28?

God works all things together, including my past damage, for good. How?

Sweet Gomer Girl, you may have endured something so awful in your past that you can't even imagine God redeeming it and restoring *shalam* to you. But His promise is true.

HOSEA

What the Enemy stole, God will *shalam*. What selfish people have taken from you, God will repay.

Faithful Job went through so much loss, but the worst of it had to be the loss of his children. You know his story, right? Well, after so much damage, Scripture says, "the LORD blessed the last part of Job's life more than the first... He also had seven sons and three daughters." (Job 42:12-13). I think it is wonderful of God to *shalam* all Job's loss, but, seven new sons and three new daughters do not replace the children Job lost. They were an added blessing, but not a replacement. At least that's the way my mom's heart feels.

I think all parents know that replacing a lost child with other children is impossible. Though a parent loves the new child like crazy, the hole in our heart from the lost child is still there. Yet the message of Job suggests God has restored all of Job's losses. Could Joel 2:25 and Hosea 2:15b speak to the same mystery?

Hosea says God will restore Gomer/Israel so they will respond as they did in their youth. Joel promises God will repay what has been taken away, making it both safe and complete. Paul says all things work for our good. Job was blessed beyond all he had lost.

Write down your thoughts and observations about what these four Scriptures have in common:

God may not *replace* what you have lost, but He will *repay* what you have lost. He will *shalam*. Look at Genesis 50:20 and speak that truth to your past damage and loss. Seriously, sister. You may even need to stand up, turn around as if you are addressing your past, and quote that truth to it.

You intended to harm me, but God intended it for good
to accomplish what is now being done... (NIV)

Good job! I am cheering you on and saying it right along with you.

Gomer Girl, you are not your past! You are not what has happened to you. You are not your struggle. You are not someone else's opinion. You are not your fear or insecurity. You are loved, accepted, and complete. You are the beloved.

So, you tell your past that it is not the boss of you. God will *shalam*—He literally will help you make peace with your past.

In my favorite C.S. Lewis book, *The Great Divorce*, the author has an imaginary conversation with one of his heroes, George MacDonald, as they sit together just outside of Heaven. MacDonald tells Lewis; " 'Son,' he said, 'ye cannot in your present state understand eternity ... That is what mortals misunderstand. They say of some temporal suffering, "No future bliss can make up for it," not knowing that Heaven, once attained, will work backwards and turn even that agony into a glory.' "[1]

What he's saying is that even your most agonizing loss, even your worst day, will be cast in the light of *shalam*—redeemed and restored as all things are made new.

Finish today by reading Hosea 6:1-3. Of what worst day and best day do those days make you think?

The "two days" and "the third day" are Hosea shouting into the future that "the Door of Hope" will swing wide open for all mankind to walk through. Jesus' death and resurrection redeem, renew, restore, and revive us!

The resurrection of Jesus reminds us that the worst day is not the last day.

"In the third day he will raise us up and we shall live in His sight" (KJV). Dear one, that literally means, "We will live before His face." And there we will stand in purity and sing as in the days of our youth.

I will trust in your unfailing love, my heart rejoices in your salvation. I will sing unto the Lord for He has been good to me.
PSALM 13:5-6 NIV

---

1. C. S. Lewis, The Great Divorce (New York, NY: Harper Collins, 1973), 69.

Day 4
MY WIFE IN RIGHTEOUSNESS

I will take you to be My wife forever.
I will take you to be My wife in righteousness,
justice, love, and compassion.
HOSEA 2:19

I've been thinking about you and praying for you as you read Hosea's words. I am trusting God's Word to be comfort and life to you. If you are broken, I am trusting God to bind your wounds with His beautiful, healing Word. Though I cannot really explain how, I believe God's restoration is so complete that it redeems the past as well as the present and future. I need that kind of redemption, especially in the areas where I feel like such a mess!

I think we all have those times or areas in our lives when we feel like a mess, right?

Let's pick up in Hosea 2:19 and see what we are to God. At this point, you don't even need to read the verse to answer this question, but here it goes anyway…

To whom does God compare us in this verse?

Note the description of God's commitment. He takes us to be His wife forever in: _____, _____, _____ and _____.

Right next to each word, write how that quality responds to sin:

Righteousness:

Love:

Justice:

Compassion:

Did you notice how those four words put together represent the perfect balance in a relationship? That is how God relates to us, with perfect balance.

Righteousness and justice point fingers of guilt and mandate sin be punished. Love and compassion cover guilt and forgive sin. Righteousness and love complete each other; justice and compassion balance each other.

Those four words describe the nature of God's covenant to you. How do you expect Him to treat you most often? With righteousness and justice, or love and compassion?

The right answer technically is "yes!" In other words, a perfect God who loves perfectly will relate to you in all those ways all at the same time all the time. We, as the imperfect recovering Iddicts we are, usually lock on to either the righteousness/justice side of God or the compassion/love side of God.

To which side do you most often gravitate in your relationship with God?

Here's the deal with most of us Gomer Girls. We either gravitate toward the righteous/justice side of God and decide we are just plain unworthy and worthless—pond scum beyond the reach of grace. Or, we lean so hard into the compassion/love side of God that we think we are just fine, everything's good, sin isn't a big deal—beyond the need of grace.

Even though this is a big no no, I want you to compare yourself to someone else.

Where do you usually think you are on the continuum from "The Worst Pond Scum Ever" to "Practically Perfect in Every Way"? The Worst Pond Scum Ever means we feel we are totally beyond the reach of God's grace. Practically Perfect means that we feel we are beyond the need of God's grace.

On the Grace Scale below, place an "M" (that means you) on the spot which best represents where you are most of the time. Don't overthink it, just estimate.

1	2	3	4	5	6	7	8	9	10
WORST POND SCUM EVER							PRACTICALLY PERFECT		

Now think of our girl Gomer. Place a "G" for Gomer on the spot which best represents where she was most of the time.

Now glance where you placed yourself and where you placed Gomer. Let me ask you some questions.

> Do you find yourself moving back and forth on that scale based on your behavior?
>
> What are some of the behaviors causing you to move back and forth on the continuum?
>
> Do you think Gomer should have been nestled up right next to Practically Perfect when she was a chaste, faithful bride?
>
> Do you think she should have been in the negatives, below pond scum, when she was committing adultery?
>
> Was Gomer beyond the reach of grace?

Romans 3:23 says "all" have sinned. The "Practically Perfect" and Gomer alike. Their sins may be different, but their condition is the same—sinners who need grace. No one is beyond the need, or reach, of grace. Our behavior isn't what dictates where we land on the grace scale.

Israel got a little full of themselves in Hosea's day and thought they were good.

> Read Hosea 5:5,11 and Hosea 7:10. Based on those verses, where do you think they would fall on the grace scale above? Why?

They were prideful and stumbling in their sin. They were determined to follow man's way, their own way. They were arrogant and unwilling to turn to God. When one behaves as they did, you may assume that they should be with the pond scum on the grace scale. You know, "we are so bad we are beyond reach of grace." But, the thing is, behavior doesn't determine where we place ourselves on that scale. Israel could have put themselves up there as "Practically Perfect" as far as not needing grace because they were prideful, arrogant, and thought they were good. After all, they worshiped Yahweh along with Baal. They were His chosen people... blah, blah, blah.

The point is they were not so bad that God could not, or would not, reach them. No one can be so good that they do not need to be reached by God's grace.

I set you up with that scale. Anywhere you marked on that scale would not reflect your true condition. If you, Gomer, Israel, or I marked pond scum or Practically Perfect on the grace scale it reflects we are deceived.

> Find Hosea 10:13. What is the reason Israel was deceived? Hint: look at the last phrase.

Hosea said they had planted wickedness, reaped evil, and eaten the fruit of deception because they had depended on their own strength. When we depend on our own strength, the ultimate result is deception. We slip into Gomerisms and trust our wisdom that tells us we are beyond the need, or reach, of grace.

Here is your choice: Depend on grace or depend on self.

We were saved by grace. But until we live "saved" by grace we will never really experience the perfect, unfailing love of God—balanced in righteousness and love; justice, and compassion.

God has chosen to betroth Himself to you in righteousness forever; love, justice and compassion are yours. Not because you earn or deserve them. You get them because God gives it. Grace.

> Which of those words mean the most to you and why? (forever, righteousness, justice, love, or compassion)

All of those words point in the same direction. They point to Jesus, "full of grace and truth."

Uh huh! And all the sisters said? Amen!

HOSEA

Day 5
RESTING IN RESTORATION

You will call Me, "My husband,"
and no longer call Me, "My Baal."
HOSEA 2:16B

We're finishing up this week and this chapter on a lovely high note. To review and get you back into context, read Hosea 2:14-23.

Everything you just read speaks to God's restoration of Israel and Hosea's restoration of Gomer. After reading those verses, how would you describe God?

What words come to mind? _____

For me, words like Redeemer and Restorer come to mind.

Now, I want you to read it again and try to glean from the verses what it is that God restored or is restoring and write it below. Don't be intimidated! If you're not used to doing Bible study this way, ask the Holy Spirit to guide you. He will. I know you can do it.

In verse 15: God is restoring

In verse 16: God is restoring

In verse 17: God is restoring

In verse 18: God is restoring

In verses 19,20: God restores

In verse 23: God restores

I'm not sure how you answered, but I love that you gave it a shot! Our answers may vary and that's OK. I will share with you my thoughts:

- In verse 15: God is restoring security and safety, joy, and hope.
- In verse 16: I think God is restoring position and dignity.
- In verse 17: It seems God is restoring purity.
- In verse 18: I see God restoring peace.
- In verses 19,20: God restores a loving relationship.
- Finally, in verse 23: I think God restores compassion and connection.

> Now, either look at your answers, or mine, and jot down what you most need God to restore in your life. Security? Joy? Hope? Loving relationship with Him? Dignity? Purity? Peace? Connection? Why?

God can restore what you lack and long for. He promised Judah and Israel He would restore them.

> What does Hosea 6:11 suggest to you?

Hosea was ministering to Israel, but, in this verse, He is addressing Judah. His words apply to Israel as well, and to me and to you too. You can see in Jeremiah 30:2-3 the same phrase about restoration applied to Israel.

> What did God say He would restore?

When you see the phrase about restoring their fortunes, you may think it means God will let His people win the lottery and get back all the money they lost when their local bank was robbed. That isn't what it means. It's better than that. That phrase is a Hebrew idiom which describes "being freed of any kind of circumstantial degradation or destruction." In other words, God will take away their indignity, shame, and humiliation.

That is how God restores you too. He not only gives back what the locusts have eaten, He restores you by preventing and removing indignity, shame, and humiliation.

HOSEA

Think about it. If you said you long for God to restore your sense of security, then as He removes your humiliation, your sense of security increases. Beautiful, huh?

God's people were like a priceless piece of silver that had forgotten its own worth and beauty. The ornate antique was tarnished and dented. It had been neglected, abused, and misused. Like a master silversmith, a restorer with a tender and skilled touch, God committed Himself to restoring them to the original beauty and glory for which they had been created. The restoration process includes cleaning, polishing, and repairing.

That means for us to experience God's restoration, we don't try to spray a pretty fragrance over what stinks in our lives, nor do we throw a bright white robe over the dirt that clings to us. Rather, to be restored, we receive correction if need be.

The restoration process doesn't always feel good. In fact, what does Hosea 6:1-3 suggest to you about the process? Describe any aspects you see in the passage.

Hosea acknowledges that God has torn, but He will heal; He has broken, but He will bind up. Just like a furniture restorer sands and disassembles just to make the piece fit for restoration to its original state, God does the same. He did it for Israel and He does it for us. In the restoration process, humiliation and indignity are wiped away. Layers of shame are removed and more and more beauty is revealed. But just like a physical restoration, the process includes a lot of discomfort, some abrasion, and a willingess to submit to the hand of the craftsman.

Hosea removed Gomer's chains, set boundaries, and brought his wife home.

She was not only redeemed, but she was restored to her rightful position. Her shame and indignity were covered by his grace and acceptance. God wants to restore you in the same way.

Gomer Girl, can you rest in God's restoration? Will you let Him clean and repair, restoring you to your beauty and intended purpose?

If so, here is the response of Israel that you can echo.

It's at the end of Hosea's prophecy. Hosea 14 begins with a call to repentance and gives words to pray. The people of Israel needed to seek God's grace and forgiveness. They needed to denounce their self-reliance and dependence on Assyria.

Their repentance was the beginning of their restoration. Read and meditate on Hosea 14 and pray those words to the Lord for your restoration also.

Israel, return to Yahweh your God,
for you have stumbled in your sin.
Take words of repentance with you
and return to the LORD.
Say to Him: "Forgive all our sin
and accept what is good,
so that we may repay You
with praise from our lips.
Assyria will not save us,
we will not ride on horses,
and we will no longer proclaim, 'Our gods!'
to the work of our hands.
For the fatherless receives compassion in You."
HOSEA 14:1-3

Well, sister, we are halfway through our study of this wonderful book of Scripture—halfway along with my new favorite prophet and his wife, one of my new BFFs! Bless you as you continue to grow through the Book of Hosea.

Remember, it is His love that makes you lovely. By faith, choose to embrace your identity—the loved, accepted, complete beloved of God.

Group Session 4

BEFORE THE VIDEO
Welcome and Prayer

VIDEO NOTES
Lose the Gomerisms

Everything Gomer was leaving Hosea to get, she _____ had.

Incorrect _____ leads us to corrupt actions.

Colossians 3:2 tells us to "set our _____ on things above" just as we would write something on drying cement.

According to Colossians 3:2, to *phroneo* means "to consistently keep your _____ focused on the Lord."

To *phroneo* means you are more into the _____ than you are into the world.

"Gomerisms" are

my _____.

my _____.

my _____.

Every time you think, "_____ way" you should think, "_____ way."

CONVERSATION GUIDE
Video 4 and Week 3 Homework

DAY 1: What significance do you see in the price Hosea paid to ransom Gomer?

How difficult do you find it to internalize the value 1 Peter 1:18-19 places on you?

How does the fact that Jesus allowed Himself to be sold for the price of a slave feel to you? How about that He connected His value to that of a woman?

DAY 2: How does it feel to be betrayed?

What memories would you relate as your Valley of Achor?

DAY 3: How does Joel's promise to make past damage both safe and complete add to your understanding or appreciation of Romans 8:28?

How does the promise that God will restore the losses of your past impact you?

DAY 4: How do you most often expect God to treat you, with righteousness and justice, or love and compassion?

Which of the words mean the most to you and why: *forever, righteousness, justice, love,* or *compassion*?

DAY 5: How do you relate to the discussion of God restoring us? What has He restored for you, or what do you desire for Him to restore?

HOSEA

Here is your choice: Depend on grace or depend on self.
#HoseaStudy

WEEK FOUR

RETURNING TO YOUR FIRST LOVE

HOSEA

Day 1
GOD ACCEPTS RETURNS

I said to her, "You must live with me many days. Don't be promiscuous
or belong to any man, and I will act the same way toward you."
HOSEA 3:3

Hey, we've now been through the first three chapters of Hosea and, remember, I shared
with you that chapters 1-3 are Hosea's and Gomer's story, the narrative. Now, over the next
three weeks, we will study parts of Hosea's sermon in chapters 4–14.

Since there is no way we could ever cover everything in this book during our time
together, I've selected themes from the next ten chapters which will be relevant for us and
represent the message of Hosea. Since he didn't write the book in a linear fashion, we will
pop in and out of chapters in no particular order at all.

So, in case you haven't read chapters 4–14 since the first day of study,
how about you pour a cup of tea and take 20 minutes or so and read
them again? When you're done, we'll dive in.

Done? Good! First, I have a random confession to make. I have a problem … I lose
receipts. I just can't seem to keep up with them to save my life. Do you ever lose receipts?
Well, if you do, you know how hard it is to return something without one.

I've had many an embarrassing moment with a sales clerk where I explain my disap-
pearing receipts; promise I haven't used, worn, or stolen the item; and then beg profusely
for them to take it back.

Sometimes it works, sometimes not. The result really doesn't depend on my per-
suasive (or pitiful) presentation to the employee. It depends on the store's policy, or that
particular clerk's ability to show mercy.

You get where I'm going with this, right? God has a no-hassle return policy. He
accepts you like Hosea accepted Gomer. He buys you back because He wants you back.
God invites our return.

Look back at Hosea 3:3 at the start of the day and choose the word which best captures the nature of Hosea's words to Gomer.

□ he demands   □ he begs

□ he invites   □ he negotiates

□ he suggests

Hosea invited Gomer to return, and he required she remain faithful. He set the boundary of faithfulness she had to maintain, but he committed himself to do the same.

Seems like an extraordinary arrangement, doesn't it? Gomer could have said, "No way, Hosea!" She could have chosen to identify with her slave-self rather than her saved-self. Gomer could have chosen to identify with her past sin more than her present salvation. She could have refused to accept that Hosea accepted her back and, consequently, she could have refused to come back with him. The point is, we can be redeemed and restored and not return.

Freed slaves don't always return home. Because we are prone to wander, if we are not humble we can keep wandering away from God instead of walking back to Him and with Him. Israel shows us exactly what this looks like, and it ain't pretty!

To what does Hosea compare God's people in Hosea 4:16?

Yeah, not one of their finer moments, right? How would you like being compared to a stubborn calf? A stubborn calf digs in her heels and refuses to follow.

Can you think of areas in your life and/or relationship with God where you could be described as a stubborn calf?

God doesn't want to drag us back to Him like a rancher pulls a stubborn calf behind his tractor. Instead, how does 4:16 suggest He wants to treat you?

HOSEA

God wants to shepherd you like a lamb in the meadow. You may not know much about livestock, but can you think of any differences between a calf and a lamb? Does one have the reputation of being more docile and submissive than the other? Uh, yep.

Read the tender imagery of Psalm 23. I think there's a reason a sheep was the animal featured and not a stubborn calf. But, try to read it as if you were that stubborn calf rather than a lamb. You get a whole different perspective. In fact, I just had to rephrase it as if I were a stubborn calf. Now, brace yourself. I am no Hosea when it comes to poetic writing, but see what you think. And see if you can relate.

A STUBBORN CALF'S PSALM 23

The Lord is my Shepherd; I shall want my own way. He will make me lie down in green pastures, but I will keep getting up and wandering off to eat dead grass. He'll pull me to quiet waters, but I will refuse to drink. He ends up dragging me along right paths and I dig my heels in the whole way. So, when I end up in a dark valley, I am absolutely terrified because I am not sure He is with me. I think He is, but, I am so self-absorbed that all I can see is the dark. His rod and staff don't comfort me; they drive me crazy and I resent them. He prepares a table before me, but I clamp my jaws and refuse to eat. He anoints my head with oil and I buck and kick the whole time. My cup would overflow if I would just be still, but I am bent on my own way. Amazingly, His goodness and mercy still follow me all the days of my stiffed-necked life and despite myself, I will dwell in the house of the Lord forever ... but, by golly, I will choose my own room!

Oh Gomer Girl, sadly, that sounds like me sometimes. Does it ever sound like you? You see, we can be redeemed rebels, stubborn calves.

When we don't cooperate with God's redemption or restoration, we really do behave like a stubborn calf and you could go to a therapist to try to peel back layers to find out why. Or, you could read one verse in Hosea that explains it. And this one verse is the truth of God.

A single passage of Hosea gives the bottom line for Gomer's problems, Israel's problems, and our stubborn calf problems. Find it in Hosea 14:1-2.

What brings about our downfall?

Our sins have been our downfall! Not our environment, our weakness, our past, our personality, our family, nor our situation are the reason for our downfall when we are stubborn calves who need to return to God and be shepherded by Him.

It's sin. Plain and simple—sin.

So, think about it, what do you do with sin?
☐ confess my sin
☐ cover my sin
☐ ignore my sin
☐ excuse my sin
☐ repent of sin

Repentance is our humble response to sin. We repent and return; God receives and restores. I asked you on day five of last week to read and meditate on Hosea 14 but today I want you to be very specific.

What does God's Word tell us to bring with us as we return to God? (Hosea 14:2)

We are to take words with us. What specific words are we to take with us according to the last part of that verse?

God tells us exactly what He wants to hear: "Forgive all our sins and receive us graciously" (NIV). My friend, don't just fill in the blank on this one, tell God the truth about what you need forgiveness for and, then, ask Him to receive you. He will receive you and restore you just like Hosea did Gomer.

Our repentance is God's return policy! Repentance not only blesses God, it softens us. The Lord told His people to "break up their fallow ground" (Hosea 10:12 ESV) because their hearts were hard and like an unattended field, the hard soil couldn't receive healthy seed or grow a good crop. Instead, they were overrun with weeds of neglect.

If you have any hard places in your heart, break up your unplowed ground with words of repentance. For "it is time to seek the Lord until He comes and showers His righteousness on you" (Hosea 10:12, NIV). Celebrate the result of that kind of repentance and return … you will "reap the fruit of unfailing love" (Hosea 10:12, NIV)! And, oh how sweet that fruit is!

HOSEA

Day 2
GOD LOVES HIS GIRLS

But let no one dispute;
    let no one argue,
for My case is against you priests.
You will stumble by day;
    the prophet will also stumble with you by night.
HOSEA 4:4-5

So today, Gomer Girl, we are going to talk about leadership in Hosea and how God expected women to be treated. You are a leader to someone. You have influence—we all do. And, with influence, comes responsibility.

Speaking of responsibility, according to Hosea 4:4-5, what two groups does God hold particularly responsible for Israel's sorry spiritual condition?

☐ teachers   ☐ candlestick makers

☐ butchers   ☐ politicians

☐ priests   ☐ prophets

☐ bakers   ☐ wives and mothers

God was pointing out that the priests and prophets were not following God and not leading the people to God. The principle applies to you and me too. As women in our homes, moms and wives; as women in the workplace; as women leading in the church— when we do not follow God ourselves, we cannot lead others to Him. And, tragically, we automatically lead them away from Him. People do what leaders do, not what leaders say, right? So, we must walk humbly with our God in constant repent-and-return mode.

God cares about how leaders lead. Write a summary statement of God's position on leadership according to James 3:1 and James 2:1-6.

God expects leaders to take the high road in life. Leaders are not to show favoritism, but humble servanthood. God even says He will judge leaders or teachers more harshly and God was saying the same thing centuries before James even penned those words.

Look at Hosea 5:1. They had been a "snare on Mizpah" and a "net upon Tabor." OK, certainly I am not the only reader of Hosea who scratched her head when she read that, right? I had no idea what those references meant and I have a feeling you don't either, so I looked it up.

Mizpah could refer to any of several cities in Israel and Tabor was a high mountain. The words mean "watch tower" and "lofty place." These would be perfect places for hunters to perch so they could snag their prey.

What Hosea was saying to the priests and prophets is "you guys are not taking the high road, instead you are on your high horse, elevating yourself just to take advantage of those you should be serving. You have snared the people into idolatry and made them your prey by injustice."

Think about it. Leaders are placed in lofty places. They are supposed to be the watchers for the people, guarding them from harm and waywardness. But, the priests in Hosea's day had actually become the ones harming the people and leading them astray. Can you think of any supposed spiritual leaders who have done similar things in our lifetime? I bet you can. I sure can. I don't want you to note it here though. The last thing I want to do is point any fingers at anyone. I want us to look only to God and into our own hearts. Instead of pointing fingers at sorry leaders who have failed us, I want us to ask God how we can be leaders who follow Him with humility.

But I want us to be honest. Not every self-proclaimed spiritual leader is even a legitimate believer. Just like today, in ancient Israel, many people were claiming to speak for God. Jeremiah described the key mark that distinguished the false prophets from the true.

How do Isaiah 30:10 and Jeremiah 6:14 suggest you could identify the false priests and prophets?

The false prophets only had good things to say. They talked about peace and prosperity instead of sin and repentance. If you thought more deeply, especially about Jeremiah 6:14, these false teachers were like a doctor who treated cancer with aspirin and lollipops. They didn't demand the painful work of rooting out sin. Sometimes it's hard to swallow truth, but it brings us life.

HOSEA

How does it make you feel that God would be angry at the ones who would abuse their power or only superficially heal your wounds?

Oh sister, knowing that about God affirms our great value. He has your back! Nobody touches His girl without answering to Him! Have you been in a situation where you longed for a white knight to come riding in and defend you?

I remember as a girl that I could always count on my Dad to rise up and show strong and protective leadership. You may not have had a dad like that, but you do have a Heavenly Father who pays attention to how you are treated. If you long for a white knight, never forget, the lover of your soul is the King of the universe and you are His daughter.

I love the King James Version rendering of Jeremiah 6:14, "They have healed also the hurt of the daughter of my people slightly."

Doesn't it thrill your heart to realize that God expresses anger at those who mess with His daughters? Well, there's more. Let's go back to Hosea 4 and see another facet of God's love for His daughters and whom He holds responsible for their exploitation.

Read Hosea 4:14 carefully. Who does God hold most responsible for the promiscuity in the land?

Who does He specifically say He will not punish?

To understand this, we need to understand the culture of Israel at that time. Baal worship had become hugely influential in Israel. The "worship" included cult prostitution. My heart sticks in my throat to even say it, but fathers presented their daughters to Baal as temple prostitutes. The practice may have been so widespread that "a promiscuous wife" (1:2) may have been just about all that was available. To say this is a topic we'd rather not think about is putting it mildly, but we need to consider it from several angles.

Many people today have rejected God because they've heard that the Old Testament God was angry and immoral. But, in Scripture, God judged sex slavery and child sacrifice.

How does that truth impact your view of God?

I'll be honest. It makes me proud of my God. He cares about what happens to His daughters and He judges those who harm us.

> What did God command to protect women in Leviticus 20:2 and Deuteronomy 23:17?

So many people have bought the idea that God is anti-woman or that He treats us as second-class citizens. The very opposite is true. The freedom and dignity of women in our world have grown and flourished because our value as women first sprung from biblical soil. Jesus talked to the woman at the well; Jesus treated the woman caught in adultery with kindness and dignity. When Jesus was on the cross, He told John to take care of His mother. When He first appeared from that empty tomb, it was to a woman.

Women matter to God. You matter to God. Oh sister, you are loved, accepted, and complete in Him. He loves you. You are His beloved.

A PRIVATE WORD FROM MY HEART TO YOURS

Many women have suffered great shame and guilt in the area of our sexuality. Of course, we take sexual sin seriously because nothing impacts us more personally. But, if you are one of my sisters who has suffered in this area, whether through your own choices or the actions of others, read Hosea 4:14 again. Whatever else we do with this subject and this passage, let this word ring clear. God defends His daughters! He is for you, sister, including placing blame where it belongs. And if it belongs squarely with you, then hear the words Jesus spoke to the woman caught in adultery who stood alone and ashamed; "Neither do I condemn you. Go, and from now on do not sin anymore" (John 8:11).

If you are facing, or have faced, particular struggles in this area with sexual guilt and shame, please get a Bible-study buddy whom you trust and share with her your struggle. Pray with her, or maybe you even need to see a Christian counselor. I pray God guides you in this sensitive matter. We don't want to justify sin, but a lot of us sure need to stop beating ourselves black and blue over sin God has forgiven, or even over guilt that was never ours in the first place.

Pray about this issue of sexual shame. If it's not your issue, pray for a sister. If you struggle in this area, take a separate sheet of paper and write a prayer of confession, repentance, petition … whatever it is you need to say to God about this, say it. Then, destroy the paper as God destroys your shame.

Thank you, Hosea, for loving a woman whom society would declare unworthy. Thank you for seeking to redeem her from her bondage. And, thank you for declaring to the people of your culture that God is on the side of exploited women.

I keep finding more reasons to love both Hosea and His beautiful God of love. How about you, Gomer Girl?

Yeah, I know … All the sisters say, "Amen!"

SEX TRAFFICKING

The International Labor Organization estimates that globally
4.5 million people were trapped in sexual exploitation in 2014
(*http://www.polarisproject.org/human-trafficking/sex-trafficking-in-the-us*).
Praise God for those brave souls who seek to end sex
trafficking and sexual exploitation in our day. At the very least,
we need to pray for them. Let's learn more about how we
can support or get involved in ending sexual slavery.

Day 3
JUDAH GETS IN ON THE JUDGMENT

The princes of Judah are like those
who move boundary markers;
I will pour out My fury on them like water.
Ephraim is oppressed,
    crushed in judgment,
for he is determined to follow
    what is worthless.
So I am like rot to Ephraim
and like decay to the house of Judah.
When Ephraim saw his sickness
and Judah his wound,
Ephraim went to Assyria
and sent a delegation
    to the great king.
But he cannot cure you or heal your wound.
HOSEA 5:10-13

Today we're dropping in on Hosea 5. The chapter is mostly judgment on Israel for their unfaithfulness and sin. But we're going to focus on verses 10-13 and someone other than Israel is included for a change! Before we get into it, see how much you can remember from the beginning of our study, just for fun.

To whom was Hosea ministering?
☐ the Northern Kingdom
☐ the Southern Kingdom

Is Israel the Northern Kingdom or the Southern Kingdom?

Which one was more wayward? Israel or Judah?

HOSEA

OK, I'll tell you if you can't remember. Hosea preached to the Northern Kingdom of Israel and they were more wayward than their neighbor, Judah, the Southern Kingdom. So imagine a citizen of Judah accidentally strolling across the border into Israel and hearing Hosea's prophecy being read. He could lift his chin, straighten his shoulders, and feel a bit smug that his lousy neighbors to the north were being so roundly rebuked and all the while his people were doing just fine.

Imagine the man from Judah hears Hosea 5:5. What makes him smile?

Israel's pride testifies against them and they are stumbling in their sin. I imagine the man thinking, "Yep, those dirty rotten scoundrels." Then, the rest of the rebuke continues and he doesn't smile.

What makes him frown in verse 5?

Judah also stumbles with Israel! The man probably thought, *What?! I thought Hosea was just a prophet for Israel. Why is he messing with Judah? The Israelites are the ones blowing it; we aren't so bad.* But, as he is still reeling from that blow, he tunes back in to hear the rebuke for his people. Now read Hosea 5:10-13.

Hosea reminds Judah that she has her own sin to answer for before God.

What does God specifically point out about the rulers in Judah? What were they doing?

**"The princes of Judah are like those who move boundary markers."
What do you think it means to move a boundary?**

The political leaders of Judah were corrupt cheaters. They were changing property boundaries to benefit themselves. Here's the back story: When the Israelites moved into the promised land, property was allocated by families and boundaries or landmarks marked what land belonged to each tribe. God designed their economic system to protect families and inheritance rights. An Israelite family could rent out their land. But every 49 years, during the year of Jubilee (see Lev. 25), the leased out land reverted back to the original owners.

For that reason, moving a property marker, boundary line, landmark, or surveyor stake was more than just a matter of stealing. Taking advantage of others was a violation of sacred responsibility. See Deuteronomy 19:14 to understand this better. Society in Hosea's day had not just become immoral, but those in power were known to have audaciously moved boundary lines and brushed aside God's commands.

But, here's the thing. The leaders weren't just violating the people by moving physical boundaries, they were also hurting the people by moving spiritual boundaries. They were blurring the lines between what was true worship and what was false religion; shifting the boundary between right and wrong.

Even today, we have to pay close attention to the boundary lines that leaders set and shift because sometimes the shift can be slow and subtle.

What examples of boundary lines changing in America over the last few decades can you name?

For example: What was once called *abortion* is now called *choice*—that was the shifting of a boundary line. What was once called *sin* is now called *weakness*. You get the idea.

What boundary shifts can you think of?

If we are not wise and grounded in our relationship with God and His Word we can easily fall into the boundary lines that an unbelieving world draws. It's easy to depend on men, especially when they seem open-minded, wise, benevolent, or influential.

Skip to Hosea 5:13. How did Ephraim and Judah show their dependence on man?

> When Ephraim saw his sickness,
> and Judah his wound,
> Ephraim went to Assyria,
> and sent a delegation
>   to the great king.
> HOSEA 5:13A

HOSEA

Ephraim and Judah were trusting man more than God—living by man's standards more than God's standards. Israel foolishly trusted in Assyria. And, do you know who eventually conquered Israel in 922 B.C.? Yep, Assyria. They trusted their enemy more than the Lover of their soul.

According to verse 13, to whom was the king of Israel running?

They ran to King Jareb instead of the King of kings. Jareb is not a known Assyrian's name, but the name means "warrior'" I think the contrast is striking. Israel could have run to the Prince of peace and instead went for a warrior.

Hmmm … something to think about. Do we ever do that?

Look at the end of Hosea 5:13. What does it reveal about Israel and Judah getting their needs met from any other source than God Himself?

"But he cannot cure you, or heal your wound." Israel and Judah running to that king would be like you going to your congressman when you have a toothache and expecting him or her to prescribe you pain killers and pull your tooth. Senseless, right?

Well, girl, there's just not much more to say about this—depending on man more than God is not smart; it's senseless.

So, finish up by reading Hosea 7:11 and jot down what we, when we are like Israel, look like.

A senseless dove flitters and flutters about, kind of bird-brained, trying to find a place to land. When we depend on man, we fall into ever-shifting boundaries and get confused about where to place our trust. Draw a line in the sand right now with me. Let's proclaim it along with Joshua, "As for me and my family, we will worship Yahweh" (Josh. 24:15).

Day 4
WHAT YOU DON'T KNOW
CAN HURT YOU

People without discernment are doomed.
HOSEA 4:14b

Here's a familiar phrase: *Ignorantia juris non excusat.* Familiar if you are fluent in Latin or a lawyer, that is. For the rest of us though, it means that *ignorance of the law does not excuse.* The idea behind that doctrine of Roman law is that if ignorance of a law could be used as an excuse, then everyone would turn into a thick-headed adolescent boy whose most frequent answer—no matter the question—is "Uh, I dunno."

Ignorance is no excuse. Knowledge, or the lack of it, is a big deal to God and a big theme in Hosea. So, in chapter 4, God is judging the priests—the very ones responsible for spreading knowledge—for propagating a lack of knowledge among His people. God said, "My people are destroyed for lack of knowledge. Because you have rejected knowledge, I will reject you from serving as my priest. Since you have forgotten the law of your God, I will also forget your sons" (Hosea 4:6). And Hosea 4:14b says that a people without understanding will come to ruin. Rough, isn't it?

Before we unpack what God meant by rejecting and forgetting His people, let's see what a lack of knowledge looks like.

How specifically does Israel's ignorance show up in Hosea 2:8?

God is saying Israel didn't know that it was God who gave them grain, new wine, and oil. And, even more insulting, they didn't know God was the One who gave them the silver and gold that they gave to their idol.

Now look at Hosea 11:3. What did Israel/Ephraim not know in that verse?

God taught them to walk. He was the One who took them in His arms, but they didn't know God was the One who healed them.

> When you ponder those verses, do you think *know* is referring to an awareness of, or an acknowledgment of?

Several Hebrew words in Hosea represent our English word *know* or *knowledge*, but these refer to acknowledgment. His people were aware, but they didn't acknowledge.

Put yourself in God's place for a respectful, humble moment. How would you feel if you met your child's, or loved one's, needs, you taught them to walk, and they didn't acknowledge it was you who met their needs? What if they took what you gave them and gave it to another who replaced you?

> How would you feel? Hurt? Angry? Betrayed?

> In the HCSB, the word *lavished* is used in Hosea 2:8. God lavished His people with silver and gold. What has God lavished on you? Time? Health? Relationships?

> Do you really acknowledge all that He has given you? If so, how do you treat those blessings?

When we know everything we are and have is because of God, we don't sacrifice any of it to idols. Ponder that thought. Pray about how it could possibly apply to your life.

Remember how Gomer said she needed to "go after her lovers" because they gave her oil and wine, etc.? Everything she left Hosea for were the things she already had in and from him. She just didn't acknowledge it. When we don't acknowledge God, we are walking on quicksand.

> Personalize the truth of Hosea 4:6. How does a lack of knowledge of God impact you negatively? What does it destroy?

God says "My people are destroyed for lack of knowledge." For me, when I lack knowledge of God, my sense of identity and value is destroyed. When I don't know who God really is, I have no idea who I am. When I don't truly acknowledge God, my sense of security starts to wane and my confidence is slowly destroyed.

So, how did this show up in Israel's national life? Read the rest of Hosea 4:6.

> How does the last part of this verse shed light on why a lack of knowledge effected them so?

"Rejected knowledge" is parallel to "forgotten the law." If you go back and read Hosea 4:1, you get the context of the chapter which explains that Israel did not acknowledge the Lord as their God. Israel didn't just lack knowledge, they rejected it.

Because Israel had rejected knowledge (God's law), God would reject them. Because Israel had forgotten God's law, He would forget their children (meaning He would remove His blessing).

Deuteronomy 28 supports this concept that God will remove His blessing, forget to be gracious if His people disobey or blow Him off. When you read Hosea 4 with its sad laundry list of Israel's bad behavior, you see Israel's lack of knowledge was not mere ignorance, but active sin.

> Hosea 8:12 explains perfectly why Israel was so willingly ignorant and disobedient. God gave them the many things of His law, but what did they do?
> □ treated it with disrespect
> □ didn't bother reading it
> □ treated it as something foreign or alien
> □ used it to wallpaper their mobile homes

God wrote for them the many things of His law, but they regarded them as something foreign. They chose to ignore His Word. Here's what we need to internalize, my fellow Gomer: we are only ignorant of His Word when we ignore it. We are only ignorant of God when we ignore Him. Put more positively, when we acknowledge God, we will grow in knowledge of God and know God better.

How can you actively apply this biblical principle? What will you choose to do to acknowledge God more fully and therefore grow in your knowledge of Him?

Unfortunately, Israel not only ignored God's Word, they ignored Hosea's warning. They kept partying and departing from the Lord. And their active lack of knowledge led to destruction. They were eventually conquered by Assyria during Hosea's ministry. But though God judged His people, our faithful God spared a remnant and restored His relationship with them.

If we don't ignore God and acknowledge, trust, and love His Son Jesus, we are never ignorant. How does 1 Corinthians 1:30 verify what I just wrote?

You got it. Jesus Himself is the very wisdom of God. Because of Jesus, you will never be destroyed for lack of knowledge. When you have Jesus, you have the wisdom of God.

God wants you to know Him—not just know about Him, but know Him. He draws you to Himself with "cords of a man, bands of love" (Hosea 11:4, KJV).

God, the Lover of your soul, says to you sweet Gomer Girl...

I will betroth you to me forever. I will betroth you to me in righteousness and in justice, in steadfast love and in mercy. I will betroth you to me in faithfulness. And you shall know the LORD.
HOSEA 2:19-20 ESV

Day 5
DON'T GIVE AWAY
YOUR HEART

Promiscuity, wine, and new wine take away one's understanding.
HOSEA 4:11

We dove into the deep end of Hosea this week, didn't we? Some of the passages we've studied left me gasping for air! But God brings us through the deep waters to cleanse us. I hope you're experiencing some cleansing; I sure am. I feel like Hosea has come in and moved the heavy furniture, exposing the dust bunnies and all their yucky cousins.

Now He's about to mess with something really deep … our hearts.

What two things mentioned in Hosea 4:11 take away our understanding? _____ and _____.

Interesting, huh? Before we see why promiscuity and wine take away our understanding, let's understand a bit about what it means to understand. The Hebrew language has several words translated *understanding*. The word *biyn* means *to separate mentally*. It means cunning, perception, or discernment. That may be the ability to think abstractly, to see how things work together. Psalm 32:9 uses *biyn*, "Do not be like a horse or mule, without understanding."

Then the Bible uses *towbunah*, which means *intelligence of the sort that can make a logical argument.* Psalm 49:3 uses *towbunah* when it says, "My mouth speaks wisdom; my heart's meditation brings understanding."

Those Hebrew words describe wisdom involving words and abstract thought. Most of the time when the Old Testament speaks of understanding it uses one of those words. But, Hosea speaks of a different understanding. In Hosea 4:11 he uses *leb*, it means *understanding of the heart,* the center of something. Promiscuity and wine take away your heart.

What do you think that means? How can anything—not just promiscuity and wine—take your heart away?

HOSEA

I think whatever Hosea meant, it is absolutely true that there are some things that can confuse us and move the center of our being. We were made to have a love relationship with Jesus as the deepest reality in our lives. When we have that, everything else makes sense and flows from the relationship.

Hosea says certain things—in this case promiscuity and wine—can erode that very center of our being. Hosea doesn't tell us why this is so. He just says it is.

Why do you think promiscuity takes away our heart?

I don't have a definitive answer, but I have some heart-to-heart girl talk I feel I need to offer. As a sister in Christ, I want to love you with the grace and truth of Jesus so, here goes … Promiscuity means having casual or indiscriminate sexual relations with different partners before, or outside of, marriage. If you can identify with that definition on any level, then sweet friend, this is God's heart toward you: Do not give yourself away to anyone but your husband. And when you give yourself to your husband, it needs to be after the ring is on your finger! Anything else is promiscuous.

Sometimes we think that is an old-fashioned, outdated concept. I know many Christian young adults who move in together or sleep together when they are in supposedly committed relationships. But it doesn't matter how committed you are, it can still take away your heart. The simplest reason it takes away your heart is because it is sin—not just a poor choice, but sin that hurts you, reduces your value, and dishonors your future husband (even if the man you're sleeping with is to become your husband.) The Bible teaches sexual purity, but even secular studies have proven that promiscuity can lead to problems with self-concept, ineffective relationships, and even depression.

Here's the deal: Purity is never, ever a bad choice, but promiscuity always is. I think the reason promiscuity takes away your heart is because it is against God's perfect design of married love that protects your heart. Promiscuity touches places in the deepest parts of your soul that are not supposed to be taken until they are willingly given in marriage.

I am incredibly aware, and totally sympathetic that you may read this and think, "Great, I'm not a virgin and it's too late because I've given away something I can't get back." Dear one, please hear me. I wrote this for the woman who is dabbling with promiscuity, or who is ignorant to its cost. If you have made this choice in the past, please read 1 John 1:9, Romans 8:1, and Isaiah 43:18-19. Confess your sin, God will cleanse you. He does not condemn you so don't condemn yourself. Don't dwell on the past, dwell in the present truth that God makes all things new! If promiscuity has taken your heart, God can give you a new, restored one. You are loved, accepted, redeemed, and complete in Christ.

OK, sister, since I've already trampled over eggshells, let's keep on walking …

Why do you think this verse says wine, or I suppose any mood-altering substance, has the effect of taking away our heart?

Read Ephesians 5:18 to help you think through this question. How can being filled with God's Spirit can protect your heart?

Anything that impairs our ability to think clearly, or to recognize our personal dignity and value to God, will take away our hearts. Being filled with God's Spirit will never negatively impact our understanding or take away our hearts. I'm sure not promoting legalism when it comes to alcohol. I'm promoting wisdom and godliness in any choices we make. I'm less concerned about a woman's choice to drink wine (in a responsible and spiritually thoughtful way), and far more concerned about nothing taking away a woman's heart.

I guess the question is, how can Hosea's teaching on this help me to live today with Jesus as the center of my life?

Whew! Any eggshells left, or did I crush them all?

OK, let's march on. What does Hosea 4:12 say leads us astray?

What does that mean? Read Romans 8:5-7 to help you answer. (Hint: could a spirit of promiscuity and the flesh have anything in common?)

Perhaps we each need to ask ourselves the following questions:
- Is what I'm doing drawing me to, or away from, God?
- Is what I think about bringing me life and peace, or killing me and creating chaos?
- Am I led by the Spirit of God or the spirit of promiscuity?
- Do my activities "take away my heart" or enrich my soul?

More than anything, I would never want to hurt or offend you. I love you and do not in any way condemn you. I just don't want anything, or anyone, to take away your heart. You are too valuable! So, if you've blown it in any of the areas Hosea taught us today, accept God's grace. If lust starts to get the best of you, don't let it lead you astray. Let it remind you that you were made for perfect love, not cheap substitutes. If a desire for any mind- or mood-altering substance has a strong hold on you, don't beat yourself up; get yourself help. Repent and forgive yourself. Don't let a cloud of shame darken your heart.

Keep digging into God's Word and let His truth wash over you. God has not called you to be the "be-perfect," He has called you to be the "beloved"! And that you are, my sister!

Group Session 5

BEFORE THE VIDEO
Welcome and Prayer

VIDEO NOTES
Shame Off You

If the Enemy can't use shame to _____ you, he is going to catch you in the act of being _____.

We are saved by grace, but we do our best to live perfectly by our _____.

Shame makes us feel _____.

Jesus gives _____ when shame wants to isolate and accuse us.

Jesus did not _____ the woman in John 8, but He also did not _____ the woman that day.

CONVERSATION GUIDE
Video 4 and Week 3 Homework

DAY 1: What experience, if any, have you had with a "stubborn calf"? How are we like stubborn calves in our relationship with God?

DAY 2: What one trait marks false prophets? Why do you think that is so?

How do you feel about God being angry at the ones who would abuse their power or only superficially heal your wounds?

How does God's attitude of protecting women and children impact your view of Him?

DAY 3: Why are God's boundary lines so important for protecting human freedom?

How have shifting boundary lines led to a loss of freedom in our day?

DAY 4: How do you suppose God feels when we give someone or something else the credit for His loving acts toward us?

How can you actively choose to do to acknowledge God more fully and therefore grow in your knowledge of Him?

DAY 5: How can something take our heart away?

HOSEA

Purity is never, ever a bad choice, but promiscuity always is.
#HoseaStudy

IDOLS
&
IDOLO-
TRINKETS

HOSEA

Day 1
THE LIE OF IDOLATRY

When they had pasture,
they became satisfied;
they were satisfied,
and their hearts became proud.
Therefore they forgot Me.
HOSEA 13:6

Hey, Gomer Girl! This week we're going to hopscotch through some more of the sermon parts in Hosea, landing on a few different themes. Let's review the condition of Israel as we get started.

- Pagan values saturated Israel's society at every level.
- They were economically prosperous, but spiritually a wreck.
- Crime soared; people couldn't trust each other.

They were a bunch of wayward Baal worshipers. Hosea 13:6 sums up what and why they were such arrogant idolaters. Note the progression the verse reveals.

God did something for them, what was it?

They became _____.

They ended up _____.

God had provided them pasture—a place of both safety and provision. Instead of being grateful, they were satisfied, became proud, and forgot God.

Oh, but they didn't forget Baal. If God had fed, loved, and delivered them, why didn't they worship and serve Him exclusively?

I wonder if they were just covering all their bases? You know, just in case God wasn't really who He said He was, or just in case He couldn't do what He said He would do, they had another god in their back pocket. Or maybe it was because they knew who God was, but they wanted a different god—one who was more appealing and would give them power.

We may look back at them, shake our heads, and think, "How could they be that ignorant and arrogant?" But let's hold up the mirror and see Israel looking back at us. How much do we resemble them? Put down your pen and just prayerfully ponder the following questions.

> Do I trust that God is who He says He is and will do what He says He will do, or do I keep a plan B just in case?

> Do I really want God to be sovereign, or do I want to be the master of my own life?

> Now that you've considered those questions, go back and write a prayer response to God concerning each one.

We humans have been idolaters since Eden. We showcased our tendency at Mt. Sinai when Israel created a calf-god. In Hosea's day, we were still worshiping that same false god. Isaiah pleaded with Judah, just like Hosea pleaded with Israel, for us to put away our idols. Even during the Babylonian captivity, Ezekiel told Judah to—yep, you guessed it—stop worshiping idols.

But this didn't begin at Mt. Sinai. Our idolatry began in the beginning … in Genesis.

> Look at Genesis 3:1. The serpent was trying to convince Eve to eat the fruit. What question did he use to persuade her?

The serpent basically said, "Did God really say that?" It was as if he were saying, "God didn't really say that. God isn't who you think He is. God can't, or won't, do what He says He will." Our first step toward idolatry began with a lie. Eve believed the lie that God was not enough.

What other clue does Genesis 3:5 provide to help us understand this tendency toward idolatry? What did Satan suggest as a benefit of eating from the forbidden tree?

The serpent said to Eve, "In fact, God knows that when you eat it your eyes will be opened and you will be like God, knowing good and evil."

Eve believed the lie that she could be like God … her own god. The lie led to pride and the result was sin.

Eve wasn't unusual. Gomer believed the lie that her lovers gave her something Hosea wasn't. Israel believed the lie that Baal could give them rain and fertility. So to cover their bases, they worshiped Baal along with God.

We often believe the lie that God isn't enough so we trust in a plan B … just in case. You know, we trust in our own wisdom and ways. Or we believe the lie that we can do better than He can when it comes to managing our own lives.

Believing those lies leads to pride. Hosea 5:5 says that Israel's pride testifies against them. Now look at the result of Israel's pride and believing a lie.

Look at Hosea 13:2. What did they do more and more?

You could have answered a variety of ways. You could have said they sinned more and more, or you could have specified how they sinned. They continued to make idols for themselves. When you think of it, it's really the same thing.

Gomer Girl, all this applies to you and me. If you believe a lie about God, you will live pridefully and sin more and more and the result will be idolatry.

Let me show you what I mean. Just for grins, what is the middle letter of lie, pride, and sin? Yep. *I*. And, what is the first letter of idol? *I*. Yep. I don't think it's an accident that idol begins with *I*. So does another word I introduced you to in day 1 of week 2. Iddict begins with *I* also.

Eve was the first Iddict in history. She chose her way over God's way; her wisdom over God's wisdom. Essentially, she chose herself over God. That is what Iddicts do; choose self over God. That's why Iddiction leads to idolatry.

We become our own idol. We say, "My way over Thy way." "My wisdom over Thy wisdom," and "My wants over Thy wants."

Anything we set up instead of, or along with, God is an idol and when we live out of our Iddiction rather than our true identity, the result is idolatry—the idolatry of self.

Let's finish up with God's words in Hosea 8:3-4. What does Hosea say idolatry leads to?

Israel has rejected what is good;
an enemy will pursue him.

They have installed kings,
but not through Me.
They have appointed leaders,
but without my approval.
They make their silver and gold
into idols for themselves
for their own destruction.

HOSEA 8:3-4

When God is the only object of our worship, we experience delight. Anything else leads to destruction. God is very clear that we should not acknowledge any God but Him.

I have been Yahweh your God
ever since the land of Egypt.
You know no God but Me,
and no Savior exists besides me.

HOSEA 13:4

As you close the book for today, ponder this question: What does the idolatry of self destroy? My confidence? My identity? My peace?

Gomer Girl, this may be a tough thing to ponder, but it will help reveal if a lie has crept into your life.

Day 2
STEPS TO CALF MAKING

Your calf-idol is rejected, Samaria.
My anger burns against them.
How long will they be incapable of innocence?
HOSEA 8:5

Well, after I threw us all into the Idols-R-Us warehouse, you may be a little concerned about what we'll talk about today! Thank you for turning the page. Like Israel and our Gomer Girl, we have all gone after other lovers—our idols. I told you yesterday that an idol is anything we set up along with, or instead, of God.

Some think of money or status when they think of modern-day idols. An imbalanced desire for acceptance, an obsessive need for personal significance, or a selfish commitment to pleasure can also be considered idols.

Money, status, acceptance, significance, pleasure, and comfort are not bad things — they are good things. But, when a woman has an elevated desire, or need, for any of those things in order to give her identity and a sense of completeness, then they are symptoms of her true idol—herself! When a woman is living out of her Iddiction rather than her identity, she uses those good things as god things—idolotrinkets.

That wasn't a typo. I just made up the word because I don't think those are our idols, I think those point to our true idol … me. I am my idol. All the things I go for to satisfy me are just the trinkets—the evidence that I am my own idol. Make sense?

Read Hosea 8:1-8 to remind you of just how low Israel had sunk
because of their Iddiction—they resorted to a calf idol.

Imagine trading the God who created the universe for a calf. If you've ever been around a dairy, you know that's just a bad deal.

In our own ways, we are calf makers too. We need to identify our process of calf-making so we can become alert to our daily choices and mind-sets. Each thought and decision either creates an idol or confirms our identity. Let's go to Mt. Sinai to see this process. The Israelites asked Aaron to make them a god. Examine Exodus 32:1 below and try to identify the corrupt thinking. Underline what you see as faulty logic.

When the people saw that Moses delayed in coming down from the mountain, they gathered around Aaron and said to him, "Come, make us a god who will go before us because this Moses, the man who brought us up from the land of Egypt — we don't know what has happened to him!"

EXODUS 32:1

The first step for an Iddict to become an idolater is corrupt thinking. Moses had been up the mountain for less than 40 days (see Ex. 24:18) when the Israelites demanded another god. Their corrupt thinking told them they needed something they already had.

Do you have any corrupt thinking in your life? Here's another way to ask that question:

Am I seeking in someone or something else anything that I already possess in God?

When we are thinking correctly, we recognize all we need is in God, the lover of our souls, and we don't need to go anywhere else to get our needs met.

Corrupt thinking constitutes step one for idol makers. We see the second step in Exodus 32:8 below.

They have quickly turned from the way I commanded them; they have made for themselves an image of a calf. They have bowed down to it, sacrificed to it, and said, "Israel, this is your God, who brought you up from the land of Egypt."

EXODUS 32:8

HOSEA

Did the people turn against God or turn aside from Him and His ways? Idolatry doesn't require a denial of God, just a reduction of God. When we act out of our Iddiction and create an idolotrinket it isn't usually in opposition to God. Rather, we veer slightly—we broaden our gaze.

In Hosea, the Israelites never totally turned their backs on the true God. They just turned aside and added the worship of Baal. (By the way, this is called syncretism.) It was like they chose one God (Yahweh) when they were in trouble, about to be attacked by an enemy ("save us") and another god (Baal) for everyday life needs like rain and grain.

> Do you ever do that? Do you ever run to God as your crisis manager
> but trust the idol of self for the everyday provisions of your life?
> Ponder that and jot down your thoughts.

My friend, when we become our own idol and choose idolotrinkets to meet our needs, it suggests God isn't enough. Idolotrinkets imply God is not doing His job adequately. An idol competes with God because we erect it to supplement Him.

> Think about how you may be supplementing God with idolotrinkets by completing the following sentences:
>
> When I am discontent, I _____ to feel fulfilled.
> When I am unhappy, I _____ to lift my spirit.
> When I am sad, I _____ so I will feel better.
> When I am angry, I _____ to help me calm down.
> When I am insecure, I _____ to feel better about myself.
> When I feel overlooked, I _____ to help me feel I matter.

Women could complete those sentences with phrases like: "go shopping, have a glass of wine, raid the refrigerator, get on Facebook, wear something that makes me look attractive, call a friend, etc." Now, not everything you wrote is necessarily a bad thing in itself, but, when it becomes a substitute for God, or when it is your way of supplementing God, it becomes a good thing gone wrong—an idolotrinket.

OK, back to Sinai! The third step is also in Exodus 32:8.

> What did God say the people had made for themselves?

Of course, they made the famous golden calf. What does that verse say they did to, and for, it?

To have a golden calf, they had already sacrificed their gold to make it. Idols are costly. Once they sacrificed for it, they had to keep sacrificing to it. Idols require constant sacrifice. Women often sacrifice their dignity, money, time, self-esteem, allegiance, and even their standards for their idolotrinkets.

When you think of your little idols, what have you sacrificed, or are you sacrificing, to keep serving them?

Let me list the steps so far:
    Step one: Corrupt thinking.
    Step two: Turning aside from God's ways.
    Step three: Sacrificing to and for the idols.

It makes sense that this is how it happens, doesn't it? Now, step four: at the end of verse 8, Yahweh quotes His wayward people.

Fill in the blanks. He said they said: "This is your _____ who _____
_____ Egypt."

The last step in idol making is giving God-like qualities to the idol. Once the golden calf was created, the people gave it credit for bringing them up from the land of Egypt. Was an inanimate golden calf that had just been created actually the one who "brought them up from the land of Egypt"? That's laughable.

Of course, a golden calf didn't pull the Israelites on a sled out of Egypt. Just as your credit card, children's success, the acceptance of others, great body, or career are not what give you peace and identity. But, when we are Iddicts, we give our idolotrinkets credit for what God does.

Look back at Exodus 32:1. When the people asked Aaron to make a god, what did they say they wanted that god to do for them?

117

HOSEA

The people wanted a god who "would go before" them. Isn't that what they said? But when the calf was created, they didn't say, "This is the god who will go before us." Instead they said, "This is the god who delivered us from Egypt." Their thinking was so corrupted that they couldn't even remember what they wanted in the first place. I understand that. I've been there. Haven't you? Are you there right now?

The Israelites didn't put their hope for the future in their idol. Instead, they gave the idol credit for their past. When Gomer gravitated toward her lovers, the reason was because she believed the same thing—they had done something for her or she hoped they would do something for her.

> When we erect little idols, it's because we really put our hope in them.
> Try this. Fill in the verse with your own reasoning.
> "This is your god _____ (fill in the blank with
> one of your gods), _____ (your name), who brings you
> _____."

Gomer could have said, "This attention from a man is your god, Gomer, who brought you out of your boredom or low self-esteem."

When I fill in those blanks, it really helps me clarify what I go to for relief, identity, or happiness. It's a painfully good exercise so really take it seriously. I want to fill in that first blank with God alone because He is my all in all; don't you?

Deep down, we know better than to say, "This is one of your gods who will go before you." But I think we get nostalgic and think, "Oh, it was so much better then." Or, "If I could just be that thin now." Or, "If I was still a stay-at-home mom."

Those were my gods who brought me out of my identity crisis, my depression, my low self-esteem, or my boredom. But, deep down, we know those idolotrinkets can't carry us into the future we long for. In the core of our souls we sense that only God, the one true God, can bring us true joy and satisfaction.

Ponder this and pray about what you are sensing from the Lord. Tomorrow, we will do some idolotrinket identification.

So, buckle up, Gomer Girl, the sisters are getting free!

Day 3
SIX D'S FOR IDENTIFYING IDOLOTRINKETS

We will no longer proclaim, 'Our gods!'
to the work of our hands.
HOSEA 14:3B

If we have seen anything in the book of Hosea so far, it is this: Iddiction is never a substitute for identity. Lust is never a substitute for love. A golden calf is no substitute for God. We will never be satisfied by the objects of our Iddictions because they are not God.

So, today, sweet Gomer Girl, we are going to be just plain gut-honest! We've got to do some hard work getting real about our idolotrinkets. I've developed the following six "D's" to identify our idolotrinkets: desire, dwell, defend, dedicate, deny, and depend.

Before you start, pause and pray. Ask God to guide you into truth. Ask Him to make His voice clear to you and shut your ears to the ugly voice of the Enemy who wants to make you feel guilty and condemned. I have prayed for you as you explore these six D's. So, pray and then pour yourself some coffee and let the idolotrinket identification begin!

1. DESIRE: Think about what you really want. You want it so badly you can't imagine not having it. It may be something you have, but you feel a tinge of fear when you think of losing it. I said we were in for some difficult work. In each of the following categories ask yourself, *If I had to choose between faithfulness to Jesus and that person or thing, would the struggle be difficult for me?* Journal your thoughts in each area.

   a. People: One (or more) person impossible to live without.

HOSEA

b. Security: Safety and protection you can't bear to be lacking.

c. Acceptance: Something that represents essential approval.

d. Identity: Does who you are depend on this?

e. Appearance: Need I say more?

Ask yourself, is something that you desire creating an idol to which you're bound? If you can't do without it, it may be an idolotrinket.

2. DWELL: Ask yourself, "Do my thoughts create an idol or confirm my identity?" What do you think about an excessive amount of time? What do you dwell on? It's less like day dreaming about how much you love and want it, and more like you dwell on how to get it, do it, have it, or what it would be like if you lost it.

On what do your thoughts most often dwell?

Whatever we think about most is, in effect, serving as our god. If we are always on our minds ... bingo! You understand why we can so easily turn into our own idol. Then your thoughts gravitate to things, people, situations, and objects that soothe you, please you, identify you, affirm you. Those are the idolotrinkets. Your thoughts stray in the direction of your idolotrinket.

3. DEFEND: Ask yourself, "If someone questions this thing I have, want, or do, am I offended or threatened? Do I defend my obsession?"

Do you tend to defend, make excuses for something, or justify your actions? If so, for what?

"It's not so bad." "It could be worse." "Everybody's doing it." "I deserve this." If you use those kinds of rationalizations, you're probably dealing with an idolotrinket.

4. DEDICATE: Ask yourself, "What am I dedicated to?" It's what you do, how you think, part of you.

What in your life do you find a way to make happen, even if it requires secrecy or sacrifice?

Midnight eating, stashing away cash, hiding what you read or watch … whatever it takes. Those just might be clues to your idolotrinket.

5. DENY BEHAVIOR: Ask yourself, "If people notice or question me, do I deny what I am doing, thinking about, or wanting?" That indicates an idol.

This is between you and the Father. Write in code if you need to, but what are you afraid others will find out?

Sweet Gomer Girl, we're as sick as our secrets. We won't hide something if we have nothing to hide. What you're hiding might be an idolotrinket. I'll be gut-honest, it was this particular "D" that helped me the most in identifying my most powerful idolotrinket.

HOSEA

And, now that God has shown me this, with His grace and strength, my view of it and, attachment to it, is changing. Note this though, often our idolotrinkets are habits that take time to break and replace, so rely on God and be patient with yourself.

6. DEPEND: Ask yourself, "On what do I depend to make me feel complete or OK?"

On what do you depend?

What does that tell you?

If you feel you need it to complete you, it is an idolotrinket. What in your life may be your idolotrinkets? Remember, they do not have to be animate objects like food or money. They don't have to be visible. Sometimes the most powerful idolotrinkets are the ones no one can see. Popularity, perfectionism, the impression you make on others, or your need for acceptance are all idolotrinkets that demand your attention when you give them power in your life.

When you think of your idolotrinkets, do they satisfy you? Do they deliver what you want from them? Why or why not?

I doubt it. The answer will eventually be a big fat NO because, eventually, the party ends, the fruit gets rotten. You may not be there yet.

When I first started writing this Bible study, I discovered I was getting overly obsessed with social media. I was basing my identity and acceptance on my number of friends, shares, and comments on Facebook. That need for popularity and acceptance revealed that I was an Iddict who had become my own idol—and all the silly social media stuff had become idolotrinkets. Little masters who demanded I be the best, the smartest, the cutest, and the most popular to feel like I had value. But that idolotrinket would eventually whisper to me, "not good enough." I had elevated my need to be accepted so high that it had become my idolotrinket. And idols are mean gods.

They are never satisfied or pleased.

And they never satisfy or please us.

Do you know why the idolotrinket has such a short shelf-life when it comes to making you happy? The answer is painfully simple. Your idolotrinket isn't God. That is what Hosea wrote in chapter 8 as he pleaded with Israel to return to their true God.

He said, "They make … idols for themselves for their own destruction … This thing is from Israel—a craftsman made it, and it is not God" (Hosea 8:4,6).

"It is not God." The most profound statement about our idolotrinkets and ourselves. They are not God and we are not God, but we treat those idolotrinkets like they are worthy of our attention and affection. We look to them to give us identity and security.

We don't worship ourselves and our idolotrinkets because we esteem them so highly. We do it because we esteem ourselves, our true identity, and the one true God so lowly.

You are too valuable to give yourself to a shallow, selfish idol who will never meet your needs. And our God deserves more, doesn't He?

Oh Lord, hear our prayer. You are the Lover of our souls, the Lifter of our heads. You are the only true God. We choose You over ourselves and our silly mini-gods. Forgive us.

We will never again say 'Our gods'
to what our own hands have made,
for in you the fatherless find compassion.
HOSEA 14:3B NIV

Amen.

Day 4
PICTURES OF IDDICTION

Ephraim has allowed himself to get mixed up with the nations.
Ephraim is unturned bread baked on a griddle.
HOSEA 7:8

Hey, today we're stepping off the idolotrinket path and exploring epigrams instead. Do you know what an epigram is? Here's a hint: Hosea uses them a lot. Epigrams are pithy sayings used to express an idea and chapter 7 is chock full of them. Take a minute to read the chapter and see if you can identify them.

The first one is in Hosea 7:4-7. To what does Hosea compare Israel/ Ephraim?

In Hosea's day, an oven was about three feet long. It was round, and had an opening for the smoke and flames to escape. An Israelite mama would build the fire early in the morning and it would roar out of control. But, as it died down, there would be an even heat on the bottom of the oven and she could take cakes of dough and place them on the inside of the oven walls to bake. Ephraim is like an overheated oven.

God is comparing His people to that red-hot oven early in the morning. After you've read Hosea, you probably have an idea of what they are doing that could compare to a flaming, out-of-control fire.

What do you think they are doing that is like that raging fire?

I know, I know. How do you answer that without reverting to PG-13 kind of words? The oven pictures not only Israel's sexual passion, but also their political passions. Their kings were all inflamed with treachery.

For the thirty years after King Jeroboam II died, Israel was in constant political chaos. Remember when you read Hosea 1:1 and saw all those kings listed? Well, Israel went through six kings and four of them were assassinated. (In fact, chapter 7, verses 5 and 6 probably refer to one of those assassinations.)

> All of us have the potential of getting out of control like a flaming oven. What does Galatians 5:16,19-21 suggest about our passions?

Even though we are believers, filled with God's Holy Spirit, our passions can spark and threaten to burn like an overheated oven. We can still dabble in the "works of the flesh."

Paul lists some of the "works of the flesh" as "sexual immorality, moral impurity, promiscuity, idolatry, sorcery, hatreds, strife, jealousy, outbursts of anger, selfish ambitions, dissensions, factions, envy, drunkenness, carousing, and anything similar." Wow, sounds like tiny sparks that became flaming infernos.

Paul goes on to say that if we continuously persist in that lifestyle, we will never inherit the kingdom of God. Paul is saying that if you are always like a roaring fire, constantly feeding that fire with works of the flesh without remorse, chances are, you are not filled with God's Spirit—you do not have the life of Jesus living in you. On the other hand, if some of those things Paul listed spark up in your life every now and then, you are probably occupied by God's Spirit, just not walking in His Spirit.

So, the take-away is this: When it comes to those "works of the flesh," determine if you are trying to squelch or put out that fire with the water of God's Word, or if you are feeding those fires so you burn with more passion. If you only feed the fires, Gomer Girl, you should be concerned about whether you have really been born again. That is between you and Jesus but if you've never come to Christ, I am inviting you right now. Call one of your Bible study buddies and talk to her about this. Come to Jesus. Let Him satisfy you.

We don't have to be sexually out of control to be like that flaming oven though, we can be like that oven when our emotions and drive get out of control. When are you most like an over-heated oven?

> Do you ever get so angry that you devour people like a fire out of control?

Lord, we want our hearts to burn with love for you. All night, we want our faith in you and our worship to smolder so, in the morning, our need and desire for you and your will blazes like a flaming fire within us. Amen.

> Now look at the next epigram in verses 8-10. To what does Hosea compare God's people?

Ephraim is like a half-baked pita bread! How would you like to be called "half-baked"? I don't think it's a compliment, do you? Hosea refers to how mixed up they are because

they have mixed with other nations in marriage and in economic dependence instead of trusting in God to meet their needs.

The word *mix* refers back to the Exodus meal offering. The pure flour was to be completely mixed with oil so that every teeny-weeny bit of flour was coated with oil. Do you remember what oil represents in Scripture? Oil represents the presence and power of the Holy Spirit. Hosea was saying the "flour" of their lives was mingled with dependence on Baal and other nations rather than with the oil of the Spirit.

Are there any parts of your life where you are more dependent on other sources of strength or satisfaction than God?

> How would your life be different if every moment, every thought, and every action was coated with the oil—the presence and power—of the Holy Spirit?

Oh girl, we would be on fire in all the right ways, wouldn't we? Oh Jesus, that is what we want. Holy Spirit, please saturate every part of our lives.

> OK, one last thing about this: What is also a problem with the dough mentioned in the last line of verse 8?

It's baked only on one side. One side is burnt to a crisp and the other is raw. Half-baked is like half-hearted. And, sister, Israel was half-hearted and it showed up in being double-minded.

> We all struggle with this one. How does this show up in your life?

Half-hearted believers have a "take it or leave it" kind of faith. Half-hearted followers of Jesus follow when it's convenient, easy, or benefits them. I know that the fact that you're doing this study shows you want to be a whole-hearted follower of Jesus.

Me too, Gomer Girl! So, today, let's be lit from within by the fire of our love for Jesus and serve Him with our whole hearts, OK? OK!

Day 5
BIRD BRAINS AND FAULTY BOWS

So Ephraim has become like a silly, senseless dove
they call to Egypt, and they go to Assyria.
HOSEA 7:11

We finish up this week with two more epigrams in chapter 7. To what does Hosea compare Israel in 7:11?

Israel was like a silly dove—lacking wisdom. They flitted back and forth between Assyria and Egypt; God and Baal. We do that too, don't we? When we run from our idolotrinkets to God and then back to our idolotrinkets and then to God … you get the idea. This image reminds me of being half-baked and we dealt with that yesterday so let's skip ahead.

To what does Hosea 7:16 compare Israel?

Israel was like a faulty bow—aimless and misguided! Psalm 78:57 makes the same connection. It says Israel is "warped like a faulty bow."

What do you think a faulty bow means?

A faulty bow believer is bent on her own way and wisdom. As a result, her arrows don't land where she planned.

How was Gomer's behavior like a faulty bow?

How is your behavior sometimes like a faulty bow?

We long for identity, but we land in crisis. We target acceptance, but we hit greater insecurity. Do you know what I mean? We aim for the right thing, but we keep achieving the wrong results. We find ourselves stuck in situations we wished we hadn't. Kind of like poor Gomer; she aimed for satisfaction and landed in slavery.

Often, we make choices or act in a way that seems fine at first, but ends up making us feel ashamed or stuck. For example, imagine you like to shop; you feel powerful and happy when you buy what you want. But then you can't pay the bills. Or you feel uncomfortable spending too much on the wrong things. You begin to hide your receipts. If you tell what you bought, especially with your husband, you round down. You hide purchases. You justify. Suddenly, what made you feel free is making you feel enslaved. What made you feel a buzz is making you feel ashamed. You have become a faulty bow.

Here's another example most of us girls can relate to. We feel that buzz of freedom when we eat. Eating makes us feel powerful, happy, or comforted. We nibble, munch, pig out, and we gain weight. Embarrassed, we try to eat less. We feel powerless. We start to eat in secret. We hide chocolate in the underwear drawer and cheese puffs in the guest room closet! The result? Weight gain. Shame. Suddenly what made us feel free enslaves us.

Hosea summarized this perfectly in Hosea 8:7. We sow wind, but reap a whirlwind!

You've seen a couple of my examples of faulty-bow syndrome. Describe something you think fits. Your example can come from your life or what you've seen in others.

A faulty bow can't shoot straight. Bent to go our own way, we land in places we don't want to be—places of stress, shame, and slavery to habits. But God has better for us. We all may be a faulty bow sometimes, but we don't have to be.

God is the Archer—He chose us. Out of all the possible bows in the world, He picked you and me. We are in His Hands. He has a best scenario for us. He knows what our hearts long for, and He knows how to get us there.

We are all different bows—designed and created for different purposes. Our son, Connor, has a friend who bow hunts so my limited knowledge comes from him. I know there are long bows and crossbows. If I'm a bow, I'm definitely a crossbow. You should see me before my coffee—cross—I'm one grumpy Gomer!

But the point is much bigger than my silly analogy. God has individually chosen and crafted each of us for a special purpose. He made us perfectly to be who He wants us to be—the chosen and loved woman He created.

God doesn't create faulty bows. If we choose to embrace our identity as a loved, accepted, and complete woman of God, we can be comfortable with the imperfect us. Our effectiveness and faithfulness depends on our Archer. I don't want to be a faulty bow who is too rigid—demanding my own way. Nor do I want to be a faulty bow getting bent out of shape by elevating my wants and trusting my own wisdom.

If you compare yourself to a faulty bow, do you tend to be too rigid, or do you easily get bent out of shape?

Faulty bows risk overestimating their importance or diminishing their value in the Hands of the master Archer. My friend, you are a beautiful bow in His Hand. He aims. You respond. Imagine it like this: God is the master Archer. You are the bow. Your gifts, abilities, desires, and calling are the arrows.

When we do not trust God, we become faulty bows, not faithful bows. The arrows we shoot are misguided and aimless. Our gifts go astray and we remain unfulfilled. Do you ever look at your life and think, how did I get here? When did I become this self-absorbed? How come I'm so insecure? Why do I always feel invisible? Why can't I ever feel good enough? Maybe that's because, Gomer Girl, you have become a faulty bow, bent on your own way.

Unfortunately, we resemble a faulty bow when we give into our Gomerisms. We land in places that don't fill our needs. We just feel emptier.

For Israel, their wayward ways kept them in perpetual dissatisfaction. List where their faulty bow landed them in each of these passages. Hosea 4:12

Hosea 9:4

Hosea 13:13

Like Israel, we go after our "other lovers" (our idolotrinkets) because we haven't found our identity in God and we're looking for something to esteem us. As our own idol, we try to find things to validate us. And the *I* in our Iddiction steps up and says, "I can, I can!"

But, eventually, the *I* of our Iddiction says, "Uh, never mind." We eat and still feel hunger. The bread that once brought us satisfaction begins to taste like the bread of mourners. No matter the epigram, no matter the chapter or verse in Hosea, the message is always the same. When we put God first, we have everything. When we put anything, including ourselves, before Him, we have nothing.

I know this might have been a tough week for you—it was for me. We dealt with lots of stuff about us that could have been unpleasant. But, sister, when we know truth, the truth will set us free! And the sister who the Son sets free is free indeed. So, let's live like the loved, accepted, and complete Gomers we are!

Group Session 6

BEFORE THE VIDEO
Welcome and Prayer

VIDEO NOTES
Redeem the Idolotrinkets

Gomer said,

"_____ desire other lovers."

"I _____ his offer of love."

"I disobey _____ Lord."

"I despair of _____."

An idol is _____ that replaces or reduces God.

Anything we go to to complete God will always _____ with God.

Three Symptoms of How We Can Know Something Is an "Idolotrinket"

1. We _____ our actions.

2. We _____ and justify our actions.

3. We put a lot of _____ into our actions.

The ultimate way to know if you have created an "idolotrinket" is that you have assigned "God _____" to it.

Everything we _____ we already have in God.

Ways to Redeem Your Idols Through Prayer

Incline my heart to Your testimonies, oh, Lord, and not to selfish gain.
Psalm 119:36

Delight myself in the Lord so I can see the hope to which I am called.
Psalm 37:4

Open the eyes of my heart so I can see the hope to which I am called.
Ephesians 1:18

Love you Lord with all my heart, soul, and strength.
Deuteronomy 6:5

CONVERSTION GUIDE
Video 6 and Week 5 Homework

DAY 1: Why do you think one idol leads to another (sin to sinning more and more?)

Why do you suppose the idolatry of self is so pervasive and destructive?

DAY 2: In what ways do we run to God as our crisis manager but trust the idol of self for the everyday provisions of our lives?

See activity on p. 116. How do you seek to supplement God with idolotrinkets?

What have you sacrificed to your little idols?

Share and compare your creative answers to the activity on p. 118.

DAY 3: What thing or things try to dominate you, to become your idolotrinkets?

Which of the words gets most to the heart of your idolotrinket: *desire, dwell, defend, dedicate, deny,* or *depend*?

DAY 4: How do you think your life would be different if every moment, every thought, and every action was coated with the presence and power of the Holy Spirit?

DAY 5: What example would you use to describe faulty-bow syndrome?

Do you tend to become too rigid or too easily bent out of shape?

HOSEA

CONNECT WITH JENNIFER AT
JenniferRothschild.com/Hosea

When we put God first, we have everything.
#HoseaStudy

WEEK 6

UNFAILING LOVE

HOSEA

Day 1
GOD WON'T GIVE YOU UP

> How can I give you up, Ephraim?
> How can I surrender you, Israel?
> **HOSEA 11:8A**

Can you believe we've come to our last week? If you've fallen in love with Hosea, like I have, our last week won't be enough. The best result of a Bible study is if it leaves you more eager and equipped to study the subject for yourself. I'm hoping that for the rest of your days you'll turn to Hosea for direction, reassurance, insight, and just to wonder at the God who loves us so radically and totally.

The more I learn to really know this beautiful, faithful, patient God, the more clearly I see what a Gomer I am. I see my complete unworthiness and how capable I am of blowing it. But I also have begun to accept by faith my own incredible value to Him. You and I are Gomers—loved, chosen, and redeemed. We are His beloved. His love does make us lovely and, because He is worthy, we have worth. It's a daily discipline for me to accept myself like God accepts me. How about you?

When you consider how we constantly spurn God's loving advances and disregard His compassion, His faithfulness just seems too marvelous to grasp. His commitment to Israel, even when they walked away over and over, proves His love is based on who He is, not who we are.

Have you ever had a friend, a romantic partner, or a close relation who has hurt you over and over? Most of us get to a point where we just say, "Enough!" and we're done with that person and their antics.

I remember the ugly end of a relationship in college. I thought I loved him. I guess, in many ways, I did. But, as the relationship grew, so did my awareness that he wasn't everything I thought he was. We were heading down a path toward marriage. In fact, the year I dated him, my mom got a "How to Plan a Wedding" book for her birthday! #awkward

When I arrived home from college just in time to celebrate her birthday, I was in tears because our relationship, our engagement, was over. Mom put away the wedding planning book and got out the tissue! I still had feelings for him. I wanted him to be who I thought he was so we could marry and live happily ever after. But I finally had to give him up and give up on him.

When I read Hosea 11:8, I get that sort of feeling from God. It feels like God is saying, "everything in me is saying I should give you up, but, how can I? If I do, my heart will go with you."

Read Hosea 11:1-8. God asks, "How can I surrender you?" What do you think that means? Surrender to whom? Surrender to what?

God asks Himself how He could give up on Ephraim, how He could surrender Israel. Perhaps, God was seeing past their sin and rebellion to the bitter fruit that was going to blossom and poison Israel's future and joy. As much as they deserved it, and as hurt as He was, His loving heart just didn't want to let them get what they deserved.

I'm no expert on God, or college romances, so let's ask the apostle Paul his opinion — at least on the God part. Romans 1:18-32 tells how rebelling humanity rejected God and became more and more corrupt.

What phrase do you see in Romans 1:24,26,28 that reminds you of Hosea 11:8?

Paul punctuated those verses with the phrase "God gave them up" (ESV). Like one of those water slides that continues down and down until it gives you up into a pool with all the other breathless soaking wet folks, Paul describes the descent of humanity into sin until it culminates in the trash bin of tragedy.

As you read Romans 1:29-32 below, mark the charges that, apart from Christ's forgiveness, would prompt God to give Israel up.

They were filled with all manner of unrighteousness, evil, covetousness, malice. They are full of envy, murder, strife, deceit, maliciousness. They are gossips, slanderers, and haters of God, insolent, haughty, boastful, inventors of evil, disobedient to parents, foolish, faithless, heartless, ruthless. Though they know God's decree that those who practice such things deserve to die, they not only do them but give approval to those who practice them. (Rom. 1:29-32 ESV)

Wow, sounds like Israel in the book of Hosea, doesn't it?

Now the much more difficult question. Look at Romans 1:29-32 again, and this time mark the charges that, apart from Jesus, would prompt God to give you or me up.

Gomer Girl that is our biography outside of Christ! Even though we have given in to our worst selves and practiced all manner of ungodliness, God does not give up on us nor does He give us up and give us over to our own depravity.

Turn back the pages in your imaginary photo album and glance at a picture of Gomer standing on that slave block. What do you see in her face? Does she look like she expects Hosea to have given up on her and just give her up to the consequences of her choices?

Now, use your mind's eye to see the photo of Hosea sitting in that auction. Does he look brokenhearted? Can you see him looking at the wife he chose and loved and hear him whispering the same words to himself? "Oh, Gomer, how can I give you up? How can I surrender you?"

For Hosea to surrender Gomer to the future her behavior deserved, he would be surrendering his hopes and dreams. Hosea and Gomer are such a vivid picture of God and Israel, and of God and us. God could surrender us to what we deserve, but He doesn't.

If God gave up on you or gave you up to a future without Him, what would your life be like?

God had made covenant with the people He loved and they broke it over and over. In His anger, He could've said, "Enough!" But in His mercy, love, and justice, He couldn't give them up. In His mercy, He was not willing to "surrender" them to their future without Him. For that would be no future at all.

Read Hosea 11:8 again. God refers to two distinct places. "How can I make you like _____? How can I treat you like _____?"

Admah and Zeboiim weren't old boyfriends. They were the little towns outside of Sodom and Gomorrah (see Deut. 29:23 and Gen. 10:19). Not only were the big cities of Sodom and Gomorrah destroyed, so were the smaller towns next to them. Why doesn't Hosea say "Sodom and Gomorrah," the more well-known locations? Well, there may be two reasons. One reason could be the use of Hebrew poetry that Hosea employed, but I think there is a far more meaningful reason that will bless you.

I think the second reason lies in the beautiful mind of God, He guided Hosea to mention those two towns because those are the two little, insignificant, rarely mentioned towns that were forgotten. God said He would not treat His people like Admah and Zeboiim. In other words, He won't forget you ever. To be "made like Admah and treated like Zeboiim" is not only to pass out of existence, but out of memory. To completely eradicate someone from your memory shows a cold disregard. God would not do that to His people no matter the pain they caused Him.

When my former college guy and I didn't work out, it took almost a year to get over him. So, Nancy, my roommate, in all her college senior wisdom suggested we try to forget him. She got out a pile of old magazines she was throwing away. She gave me half and instructed: "Let's go through and rip all these pages. Tear them up! Wad them up! Every page is something he did or said." We started ripping. What started as tears ended in laughter. I had totally annihilated that poor guy. Ripped him out of my heart with every tear of shiny paper. Shredded the memory of him, but of course, not really. It was just a way of dealing with sorrow and anger.

If I could have really torn him from memory he would no longer exist for me. That would be a depth of disregard he didn't deserve no matter what he may have done. God does not treat His people with disregard no matter their violation. God's grace holds Israel and will not let them be swallowed up in the flames of forgetfulness. Beautiful.

According to Hosea 11:9, why won't God destroy them?

"I will not execute my burning anger;
I will not again destroy Ephraim.
For I am God and not a man,
the Holy One in your midst."
HOSEA 11:9 ESV

God never gives up on you even if you give up on Him. He forbears, endures, forgives, and shows mercy. It's not because we are good; it is because He is God.

For us Gomer Girls, the big take-away is that God cannot, will not, chooses not, and will never forget you. He will not disregard you as if you never existed no matter what you do, or do not do. He will not surrender you to a future without Him.

As you finish up, close your eyes for just a moment and thank God for never giving up on you, or giving you up to your own sin and selfishness. Then, go live like the beloved woman you are!

Day 2
WHEN GOD WITHDRAWS

They go with their flocks and herds
to seek the LORD
but do not find Him;
He has withdrawn from them.
HOSEA 5:6

Well, Gomer Girl, yesterday I hope you leaned into the beautiful truth that God can never, and will never, forget you or give you up. But, we must take a look at another side of God Hosea presents.

Actually, it's His back side.

What horrifying reality about God does Hosea 5:6 suggest?

Hosea suggests God is withdrawing from Israel. He lists the reasons in the first 5 verses of chapter 5.

But, what does God promise in Deuteronomy 31:6 and Hebrews 13:5?

God says He will never leave nor forsake us. So since all the Bible is true, that means both statements are true yet they seem to contradict each other.

How would you seek to explain how both statements can be true?

In Hosea 4:17, God promised to leave rebellious Israel alone. If God promises His presence, how can He also promise to leave?

God said He would withdraw and leave His people. What He means is that when His people make superficial gestures of repentance, they will not find Him. He will not dignify their shallow, selfish religiosity by granting them the fullness of His presence.

> Look at how they were supposedly seeking Him in Hosea 7:14. Just for grins, doodle a picture of this verse!

I imagine them sprawled out, whining, and wailing like grown-up baby men! They were slashing themselves and crying on their beds. This is actually a picture of Baal worship, trying to get the attention of that false god, while at the same time, hoping Yahweh would tune in too.

> But, in Hosea 7:14, what did God point out about their method of seeking Him?

They couldn't find God because they weren't seeking Him with their hearts. They were half-heartedly seeking Him with theatrics and sacrifice, but not with sincerity.

God will never withdraw from relationship with His people. He made a promise, a forever promise. He does withdraw the fullness of His presence sometimes; He pulls back. The change is in proximity, not relationship.

Have you ever said, or heard someone say, "My prayers just seem to hit the ceiling"? That's kind of what Hosea is saying it will feel like for Israel if they don't repent and God withdraws. How are we like Israel?

Sometimes we say we're seeking God, but we're really seeking a spiritual experience that will satisfy us. With the potpourri of different churches and ministry styles, people can use religious activity as a means of satisfying themselves rather than seeking God. Picture this: A Gomer Girl starts out in the First Baptist Church of Israel, but she feels the drums are too loud so she goes to the Methodist church instead. The preacher at the Methodist church is too boring though, so she just can't hear from God there. Next Gomer heads over to the Pentecostal church where God speaks every Sunday. Oh, but she doesn't like the carpet color in the sanctuary and the pastor's wife didn't smile at her. Well, Gomer has to leave and try the Presbyterians. The Presbyterians have uncomfortable pews

HOSEA

and Gomer just can't get comfortable. How can she develop her relationship with God if her lower back hurts? Better head to the Episcopal Church. They have such beautiful liturgy; surely Gomer can find God in all that beauty. But, alas, the rector has an annoying lisp so she leaves for the Evangelical Free! But the Evangelical Free's music ministry isn't exciting—it doesn't even use drums, so Gomer needs to leave and go to the nondenominational church. She arrives and discovers … the drums are too loud! Poor Gomer is so frustrated because she is just trying to seek the Lord. Really? Is she seeking the Lord, or her own satisfaction?

That's what Israel was doing. They weren't seeking God. They were involved in spiritual investigation. Gomer Girl, here's the deal … When you can't find God anywhere, most likely, you aren't looking for Him. You are actually running from Him.

> What is God's guaranteed method of finding Him according to Jeremiah 29:13?

A seminary degree? Nope! A good Bible study? Nope! The right worship style? Nope! God guarantees you will find Him … if you seek Him with your whole heart.

We will find God when we seek Him with our whole hearts even if the pews are hard, the drums are too loud, the preaching is boring, or the carpet color is just plain ugly!

When we allow unimportant, non-essential trappings of our spiritual pursuits to become barriers to finding God, it points to the fact that maybe we aren't really looking for Him. We may be seeking religion with our whole hearts rather than relationship with our whole hearts.

> What do you think seeking God with your whole heart looks like?

If we, like Israel, settle for empty religion over relationship with the living God, He pulls back and leaves us to ourselves. Usually we don't even notice at first, but when things don't go our way, we start to notice God has stepped away. Hosea promised Israel that they would experience the emptiness of God's absence if they didn't repent and seek Him with their whole hearts.

> Look how Hosea 5:9 describes the sad result. He says Ephraim will be:
> ☐ disappointed ☐ desolate
> ☐ depressed ☐ delighted

In chapter 5 Hosea described what eventually happened to Israel in 722 B.C. when their enemy Assyria conquered them. They were left desolate. Desolate is a perfect and sad word to describe the state of God's withdrawal.

Can you think of a time when you felt emotionally or spiritually desolate? What was it like for you?

Can you think of the reason for that spiritual or emotional desolation? Were you seeking God with your whole heart?

Do a soul inventory. Do you invest more in your religious activity for God or in your relationship with God?

Hosea 6:6 tells us what God wants from us. What specific two things does He desire?

God said, "For I desire loyalty and not sacrifice, the knowledge of God rather than burnt offerings" (Hosea 6:6). Throughout his ministry, Hosea challenged Israel to relationship rather than religious antics. The prophet Micah deepened this challenge later on.

Read Micah 6:6-8 and identify some of the "sacrifices" or "burnt offerings" Hosea was referring to.

In what way(s) do you see the urge in yourself to bring sacrifice rather than "walk humbly with your God"? Or, I could phrase that question like this: In what ways do you see the urge in yourself to be religious rather than in relationship with your God?

HOSEA

In what ways do you think loyalty is more difficult than sacrifice?

I think those two questions get at the heart of Hosea and Micah. The prophets called for loyalty to God, heart religion born out of love for Him more than religious sacrifices that can be reduced to a to-do list.

You and I are the beloved. We are not the be-perfect or the be-better-so-you-can-perform-well-and-please God! We Gomers need to learn to just be the beloved.

That means we may need a new to-do list. As you finish up today, make a new list that has absolutely nothing to do on it! Make a to-be list! Put together a few things on a list that will help you be, just be, the beloved who whole-heartedly seeks the Lover of your soul—Jesus.

Here are a couple of examples of how you can turn your do's to be's:
1. Micah says we are to "walk humbly with our God." So, on your to-be list, you could write: "Humble companion of God"
2. Hosea says God desires our loyal love, right? So, on your to-be list, you could write: "Loyal lover of God"

Get the idea? Spend a few minutes writing your to-be list.

Once you get a few things on your list, start following your new list and ignoring your old one. It will help you seek God with your whole heart as you be the beloved!

Day 3
HEART RELIGION

Come, let us return to the LORD.
For He has torn us,
and He will heal us;
He has wounded us,
and He will bind up our wounds.
HOSEA 6:1

OK, Gomer Girl, this question will test your memory ... ready?

Can you name the first four written prophets I mentioned the first week of our study?
1. Hosea (you know him, right?)
2.
3.
4.

I've compared the four great eighth century prophets to the Beatles, who changed the music landscape forever by introducing a new style of music. Amos, Hosea, Isaiah, and Micah did the same—they introduced a new page of Scripture to the Hebrew people. Before they came along, there was only a two-part Bible—the Law and the Writings. The Law holds up the demands of God and condemns sin. The Writings primarily reflect the heart of man—from the depths of despair to the heights of worship.

The prophets blew across the landscape of Scripture with a fresh wind. Some have called it heart religion. Hosea, along with his prophet buddies, elevate the spirit of the Law and motives of the heart above mere actions. The prophets sing the high notes of God's love and the low notes of God's wrath all in the same song.

We can picture Hosea like the drummer in this prophet band. He beats the dual tempo of God's love and wrath; condemnation and compassion. Check out some of the verses we've already studied that show these contrasts:

- "I will not be your God" (1:9).
- "You will call me, 'My husband'" (2:16).

- "I will say to 'Not My People: you are my people'" (2:23).
- "I am like rot to Ephraim" (5:12).
- "My anger burns against them" (8:5).
- "When Israel was a child I loved him, and out of Egypt I called My son" (11:1).
- "I am God and not man, the Holy One among you" (11:9).

I've saved what, to me, is the most challenging of those contrasting passages for now as we draw our study near a close.

To me, Hosea 6:1 contains the most hopeful and challenging statement in the book. Write the contrasts presented in that verse:

God has _____ us and He will _____ us.

God has _____us and He will _____.

Now, read Deuteronomy 32:39. What contrasts does this verse also present about God?

Just like the description of God in Deuteronomy, Hosea makes it clear that it is God who has torn, and God who will heal. It is God who wounds and God who binds wounds.

What do you think this means? How does God both wound and heal?

Hosea is using figurative language borrowed from medical science of his day. (See Isa. 1:6.) The people knew deep down that only God could heal their wounds; and it was often by the wound He inflicted that their healing came.

Look back at Hosea 5:13. Where had they been going for healing?
□ urgent care
□ Assyria

Of course, the Israelites had run to Assyria to for deliverance, for healing. But Hosea proclaims that our God, who sometimes must tear us to heal us, holds the only real help. Hosea begged his people to return to God, for only Yahweh—not Jareb, nor any king of Assyria—is the Great Physician.

In Exodus 15:26, God assured His people that He was their Healer, not any other king, yet He often wounds to heal.

> How does the understanding that God both wounds and heals impact you personally?

Hosea proclaims that Father God has wounded us and He binds our wounds. God charges us with the penalty of our sin and He pays for it with His own Son's blood.

Have you been wounded?

> What is the greatest affliction God has placed or allowed in your life?

> Can you see how that wounding has been part of greater healing?

I wish we could sit together and I could hear your story. Sometimes, it's hard to think of our good, perfect, compassionate God actually tearing or wounding us, isn't it? But think of it like this: To restore you to health, a good surgeon will wound you or tear you to heal you. After the wounding, he binds your wounds. A surgeon doesn't wound because he is angry, he wounds because he is compassionate.

HOSEA

What would you describe as the greatest deliverance God has brought to you?

The Book of Hebrews contrasts the image of Mt. Sinai and Mt. Zion reminding us of our wounding/healing God. See how you can relate Hebrews 12:18-24 to Hosea 6:1.

Look at Hebrews 12:18-21. We first approach the Mountain of Fear. What is this experience like?

Then, we appreciate the Mountain of Joy in Hebrews 12:22-24. What is this experience like?

Just as God says He wounds to heal, we feel the crushing weight of our sin at Mt. Sinai before we experience mercy at Mt. Zion.

Oh, my friend, this is our loving, mysterious God of unfailing love. Harder than steel, He enfolds us in His tender embrace. Before you close your book today, give Him a shout of sincere, whole-hearted praise!

And If you're struggling with the wounding/healing nature of God's love for you, meditate on Proverbs 3:11-12 and Hebrews 12:6.

Day 4
THE JESUS OF HOSEA

He will revive us after two days,
and on the third day He will raise us up
so we can live in His presence.
HOSEA 6:2

Well, girl, there is so much more of Hosea and so few pages left in this study! Please, please keep studying this beautiful book—we've only scratched the surface of the deep truths in Hosea.

I have rewritten these last two days of study over and over because I wanted to tell you so much, but I had to select what I felt mattered most. And with that in mind, it was easy. Jesus matters most, so let's see Him in Hosea.

Yesterday, we looked at Hosea 6:1—the picture of the seeming conflict between the wrath and love of God. The next verse offers the veiled solution to that conflict.

What do you see hinted at in Hosea 6:2?

Hosea points to Jesus with "on the third day He will raise us up so we can live in His presence." Jesus Christ's death and resurrection is the ultimate presentation of and solution to God's wrath and love because Jesus is the ... wait for it, wait for it ... King James word alert ... Jesus is the propitiation for our sins.

Use Romans 1:18; 3:24-25 and 1 John 4:10 to explain in your own words what propitiation means.

The Israelites tried to appease their calf gods with sacrifices; they cut themselves and whined on their beds to try to appease Baal. Ancient pagan religions taught the idea that man could only satisfy a god with gifts or sacrifices. Propitiation is the act of appeasing, or satisfying, the wrath of an offended person. But man's best can never make up for our worst. Eternity in hell is the only way to appease God's righteous anger toward sin.

HOSEA

But hell means punishment and eternal separation from the God who loves us, so God Himself provided the gracious means through which His wrath can be appeased.

> In the passages you just read, who does the work of propitiation and reconciliation?
> ☐ God
> ☐ man

Hosea foretold what Jesus fulfilled—God offered the perfect sacrifice so His wrath was satisfied and we can be reconciled to Him. God does the work, we simply respond with humble faith and repentance.

> How did God express this thought in Hosea 14:4?

> Based on those beautiful words, who heals your waywardness?

> Can you heal your own waywardness?

> If God's anger has turned away from you, where has He placed His anger instead?

Hosea 14:4 hints at propitiation. We can't heal ourselves or appease God. Because of our sin, we are objects of His wrath, but He has turned His anger from us and placed it on Jesus instead.

Sweet Gomer Girl, God loves you that much. You are that significant to Him. Don't try to repair yourself—respond to the restorative repair work of God in you through Jesus. "It is God who is working in you, enabling you both to desire and to work out His good purpose" (Phil. 2:13).

> If Hosea 6:2 refers to Jesus' resurrection on the third day, how does that make us able to live in God's presence? Use Romans 6:5-11 to help formulate your answer.

Jesus' death and resurrection makes us alive to God! Centuries before Jesus walked on the dusty roads of Galilee, Hosea prophesied He would die so we could walk with Him, free from sin. Amazing!

But that isn't all.

Hosea foreshadowed Christ in other ways too. Take a look at some other point-to-Jesus passages.

Hosea 2:19 says God will take His people as His bride forever in righteousness, love, and compassion. Look at Revelation 19:7. When has, or will, God take His people as His bride forever?

Probably Hosea's most well-known messianic passage is Hosea 11:1. To what event in the Gospels does it relate? (Hint: if you need to, check Matthew 2:15).

Now, compare Hosea 13:14 and 1 Corinthians 15:54-55. What event does Hosea predict that Jesus fulfills?

I will deliver this people from the power of the grave;
    I will redeem them from death.
Where, O death, are your plagues?
    Where, O grave, is your destruction?
HOSEA 13:14, NIV

Oh, girl, Jesus redeemed you once and for all on Calvary, but He redeems you every day from the power of sin and death. He has reconciled you to God and continues to keep you through His blood every time you sin. Keep receiving His love and provision. You are no longer a slave to sin or self! Gomer Girl, we are complete, loved, and accepted women of God who are not only saved by grace but slaved by grace!

And, all the sisters said … amen and amen!

HOSEA

Day 5
LAST WORDS

Take words of repentance with you
and return to the LORD.
Say to Him: "Forgive all our sin
and accept what is good,
so that we may repay You
with praise from our lips."
HOSEA 14:2

When I'm near the end of a great fiction book, a dread comes over me because I don't want to finish. I will miss the characters and my time with them. That may sound weird to you, but it may make total sense because you may feel that way about finishing Hosea—I sure do. I will miss my friends Gomer and Hosea, won't you?

Turn back to Week 1, Day 2 and review the words you wrote about how you perceived God based on your first reading of Hosea.

Now, jot down your impression of God after studying Hosea.

Have your adjectives changed? Even if they haven't, I hope you have. I hope you've tasted God's unfailing love and His love has changed you.

Hosea's book probably represents a lifetime of preaching rather than a single sermon. But the Book of Hosea is definitely a sermon.

And now we come to the end. Israel had sown the wind. The whirlwind was coming, but they would also be swept up by God's love and grace. Let's hear Hosea's closing words to his sermon.

Read the last chapter, Hosea 14.

Hosea opens with a final appeal for Israel to return to God and he bluntly says they have stumbled in their sin.

But, in verse 2, how does he say they should return?
☐ with sacrifices
☐ with words
☐ with better goals

Hosea tells them (and us) to take words of repentance with them.
What exact words does God desire from them?

For what sins do you think Hosea was pleading for Israel to ask forgiveness?

Idolatry, dependence on foreign power, promiscuity—the list could go on and on. But, since we are Israel and Gomer, we need to personalize this passage. When you start to stray from your first love, return, and take words with you just as God asked of Israel. He doesn't want sacrifices or excuses, He wants our humble return and repentance.

Are there any words you need to say to God as we finish this study? If so, read over 2 Corinthians 7:10-12 as you consider what you need to say to Him. Write your prayer below.

Dear God,

Amen

HOSEA

When we come with words of repentance, God forgives and restores. (See Hosea 14:5-6.) Like withered vines receiving new life after a rain, the dew of God's mercy revives us and makes us blossom to our beautiful potential.

Hosea spoke words to Gomer in Hosea 3:3 when he walked her off the slave block. Read them to refresh your memory. I just wonder if he could have said more to her. Perhaps he whispered in her ear and if he did, maybe it sounded something like the following. And when you stray, feel enslaved by sin, or regretful for your own idolatry, read these words and take them as spoken to your heart.

"Gomer, don't be afraid, I am here. Don't let shame keep you from turning to me. I don't see what you've done; I see who you are—my beloved bride.

"Even when you're stained and tattered, you have my heart.

"Though I feel hurt and angry, I will never leave you. I will always be yours even when you don't want to be mine.

"You may see my anger and disappointment, but my anger is born of love—deep, relentless love for you. I don't love you because of anything you have done. You cannot merit my love and you can't forfeit it either.

"My beloved, my affection toward you is stronger than the chains you once wore. I willingly bore your shame when I redeemed you and you now bear my name. How can I give you up?

"You were the bride I chose and you will always be the bride I love. When I loved you, your loveliness rose in you like the sun. You blossomed and became the beautiful bride I knew you always were. The wilderness was no place for you. Let the water of my words refresh and bring you back to life.

"I see your secrets. I know your fears. Nothing you have done is hidden from me; I have felt each choice as a dagger in my heart. If I did not love you so, you could not hurt me so. But the sorrow I feel from your rejection is never so great to make me forget you. Your sin is ever before me, but so is your suffering, your fragility, and your naïveté.

"Come home, my beloved. You are the bride. You were clothed with a radiant gown of purity and it still fits you. Let me help you remove the ragged garment of your rebellion. It does not bring out your beauty.

"You rejected my provision and went to other lovers to get your needs met. You rejected the position of honor I placed you in and went to other places and people to find your prominence. You haven't behaved like the beloved bride I chose, but you still are my beloved bride.

"Do you only want love you can earn? Do you only desire worth that you feel you deserve? Maybe you only think you are significant if you have achieved your own importance.

"Gomer, you are worthy and significant. I love and accept you and when you embrace that truth, you will find the completeness you long for.

"You have been trying to become who you already were. You have been striving for what you already possess. You have been seeking what was already yours. Return with me … return to me. Reclaim what is yours in me. I have pulled you toward me with cords of love, not chains of condemnation. I don't want you to wear that yoke of slavery when you should be clothed in the garment of a beloved bride.

"You are worth the cost of this redemption to me. I will always see you as beautiful for you are mine. I will always think of you as lovable because I love you.

"Cease striving to find your place, my precious Gomer; you are already found in me."

Can you just let those words settle over you? Can you hear those words as God's words to you? Linger here and internalize His affection for you.

My fellow Gomer, I want to leave you at this scene by yourself … just you and God. But I guess we need to say good-bye first.

We will have to wait until we gather for coffee in the New Jerusalem to know the rest of Gomer's story. But I believe Hosea and Gomer worked it out. Deep in my heart, I hope she "stayed with him many days" as he asked in Hosea 3:3. I think Hosea's love ultimately overcame Gomer's wayward heart just like God's unfailing love overcomes ours.

Hosea's strong love for Gomer was but a tiny sliver of Christ's unchanging, unbreakable, unconditional, unimaginable, and unfailing love for you.

And, Sweet Gomer Girl, His unfailing love really does change everything.

Praise You, Lord!

Fellow Gomer Girl, thanks for joining me, Hosea, Gomer, and God for these past few weeks. My prayer as we part for a while is that Hosea will be a blessing to you all your days. Please visit me at *www.jenniferrothschild.com* and drop me a note about how God is blessing and changing you through Hosea. Sister, your words will bless and change me.

Until then,

Jennifer

Group Session 7

BEFORE THE VIDEO
Welcome and Prayer

VIDEO NOTES
His Boundary of Love

Whom God redeems, He _____.

God wants us to see Him as the lover of our _____.

God draws each of us with the cords of love of the Son of
Man, _____ _____, to Himself.

Hosea drew _____ which were an expression of _____.

The Hebrew word in Hosea 11:4 for *cords* is the same as the word for _____ in
Psalm 16:6.

The boundaries of love that God places in our lives are the cords of love that He uses to
keep us _____ to Him so that we will be _____ in Him.

Cords of Love in the Book of Hosea

       The cord of _____ (Hosea 5:15)

       The cord of _____ (Hosea 2:7)

CONVERSATION GUIDE
Video 7 and Week 6 Homework

DAY 1: What do you think it means for God to "give you up"? If God gave up on you, what would your life be like?

What significance do you see in Hosea 11:9?

DAY 2: What do you think seeking God with your whole heart looks like?

What items do you think go well on our "to be" list?

DAY 3: What do you think it means that God both wounds and heals us?

How has God used your greatest wounding to bring the greatest healing in your life?

How has Hosea helped you to appreciate both the mountain of fear and of joy in your relationship with God?

DAY 4: What does *propitiation* mean? How have you seen people trying to make propitiation for themselves?

How does Jesus' resurrection on the third day make us capable of living in God's presence?

DAY 5: What do you think it means that God doesn't want our sacrifices or excuses, He wants our humble return and repentance?

What one thing do you value most from your study of Hosea?

HOSEA

LEADER TIPS AND LOVE GIFTS

Session One: Ingredients in Hosea

OPTIONAL LOVE GIFT: Since I shared about making mints, I provided the mint recipe on *www.jenniferrothschild.com/hosea* for you to print and give to each group member. For extra fun, you could either make the mints or have group members make mints together.

OPTIONAL LEADER TIP: The women in your group may enjoy my book, *Invisible: How You Feel Is Not Who You Are*. It invites women to experience a more imaginative version of Gomer's life. The reader can attend Gomer's wedding, watch her as a new mom and even stand on the slave block with her. *Invisible* is a complement to the Hosea Bible Study, not a requirement. You can learn more at *www.jenniferrothschild.com/hosea*.

Session Two: When You Say "I Do" to I Am

OPTIONAL LEADER TIP: Provide mirrors or ask women to find one in their purse. Challenge your women to look into a mirror and say, "You are loved, accepted, and complete," or replace the word "you" with your name. This will reinforce the truth about who they are. To enhance connection with each other, the women could speak those truths to each other in the group setting. Some women have never had someone look them in their eyes and tell them they are loved and accepted. You can also ask the women to pick a buddy and text her those truths during the week. This will help remind her that she does not "lac" anything in Christ.

OPTIONAL LEADER TIP: What you experienced on this week's video is captured in print in *Invisible*, chapter 3, "When You Say I Do to I Am." Group members can use the *Invisible* book to minister this truth to other women who aren't a part of the *Hosea* study.

Session Three: When You Ain't Got Yada, You Ain't Got Nada

OPTIONAL LOVE GIFT: Go to *www.jenniferrothschild.com/hosea* for a "press on" printable for each member of your group. (Printing this on cardstock will make a nice presentation.) Ask her to put it in her Bible, on her mirror, refrigerator, or dashboard—wherever it will be most obvious to her so she can be constantly reminded to *yada* God—to press on to know Him. This will also help her memorize and meditate upon Hosea 6:3.

OPTIONAL LEADER TIP: Chapter 14 in *Invisible: How You Feel Is Not Who You Are* ends with a moving story which reminds us that when we have Jesus, we have everything. If you have the *Invisible* book, consider reading aloud the closing story entitled, "When You Have the Son, You Have Everything" as a meaningful way to close this session.

Session Four: Lose the Gomerisms

OPTIONAL LOVE GIFT: Go to *www.jenniferrothschild.com/hosea* and print a set of "I truth" cards for each woman to confess. This will help her to "set" her heart on truth and "cement" those truths into her mind. Just for fun, you, or a group member, could purchase inexpensive white organza jewelry bags to insert "I truth" cards into for each member. The white bags represent their new and true identity as a pure, beloved bride of Christ.

Session Five: Shame Off You

OPTIONAL LOVE GIFT: Provide two medium-sized, smooth rocks and a Sharpie for each woman. Ask her to write on one of the rocks what she has been condemning herself for. Then, ask women to drop those rocks of condemnation, and pick up "grace" rocks instead. (If you prefer, instead of a rock, you can ask women to write on paper what they have condemned themselves for and then wad it up and throw it away.) Then, on the second rock, the "grace" rock, ask them to write *grace, forgiven, accepted* or whatever they need to receive and personalize from God. When they are tempted to pick up rocks of condemnation, ask them to pick up their "grace" rock instead. Read them Psalm 61:2 as a reminder of what to do when they feel overwhelmed.

Session Six: Redeeming the Idolotrinkets

OPTIONAL LOVE GIFT: Print out the "Idol-Busting Prayer" found on *www.jenniferrothschild.com/hosea* and give one to each group member. Encourage each woman to use this as a prayer guide as she identifies her idolotrinkets and seeks to break their power.
OPTIONAL LEADER TIP: For extra insight into this subject of idolotrinkets, you may want to recommend members read chapter 9 and 10 in my *Invisible* book.

Session Seven: His Boundary of Love

OPTIONAL LEADER TIP: Challenge women to choose a boundary that will help keep them close to God and protect them from straying from their true identity in Him. Remind them that boundaries are not prisons; they are pleasant places that provide protection. If they feel comfortable, ask them to share with their Bible study buddy their boundary so their buddy can pray with and for them.
OPTIONAL LOVE GIFT: Purchase, or ask each woman to purchase inexpensive jewelry cords. Fashion them—or find a crafty woman to fashion them into necklaces or bracelets—this can be as expensive or inexpensive, as elaborate or simple as you choose. An inexpensive metal band (a ring) could be strung on the cord to represent "bands of love and cords of a man." (Hosea 11:4) This can be a sweet way to end the study and it will serve as a reminder that God draws them to Himself every moment of every day with bands of love and cords of a man.

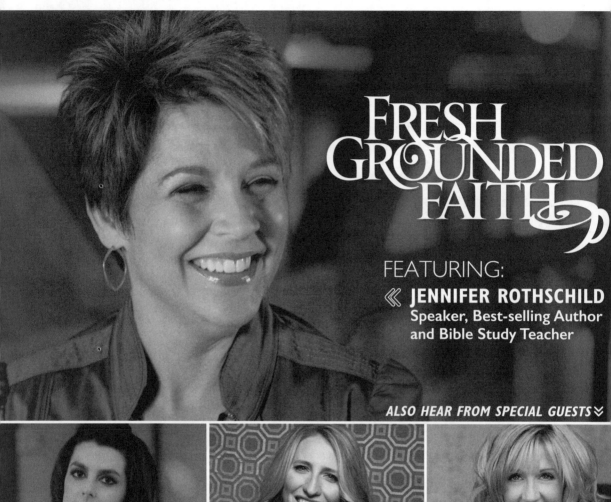

BRING FRESH GROUNDED FAITH TO YOUR CHURCH!

FRESH GROUNDED FAITH

FEATURING:

« **JENNIFER ROTHSCHILD**
Speaker, Best-selling Author
and Bible Study Teacher

ALSO HEAR FROM SPECIAL GUESTS »

MEREDITH ANDREWS

LAURA STORY

ANGELA THOMAS

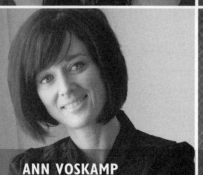

ANN VOSKAMP

STORMIE OMARTIAN

LYSA TERKEURST

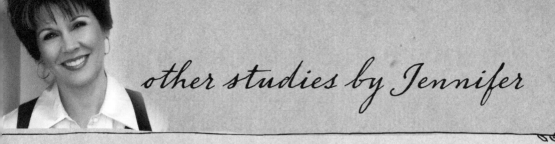

other studies by Jennifer

MISSING PIECES: REAL HOPE WHEN LIFE DOESN'T MAKE SENSE

7 sessions

Does God care? Is He fair? Is He even there? Although you may know all the right answers, they don't always feel right. Explore these and other questions in this realistic look at the messy, mysterious uncertainties of faith. God's ways don't always make sense, but He is trustworthy. Come close to Him. Experience unexpected peace despite your heartache. Trust Him more than your feelings. God will reveal Himself to you and fill in your missing pieces.

Member Book	005371621	$12.99
Leader Kit	005371622	$149.99

Contains DVDs and Member Book with leader helps

ME, MYSELF & LIES: A THOUGHT CLOSET MAKEOVER

7 sessions

Encourages women to replace the negative thoughts in their minds related to things like self-esteem, body image, and stress with positive truths from God's Word.

Member Book	005179845	$11.99
Leader Kit	005178627	$149.99

Contains DVDs and Member Book with leader helps

lifeway.com/jenniferrothschild
800.458.2772 | LifeWay Christian Stores

Pricing and availability subject to change without notice.

LifeWay | Women